API ECONOMY 101

JARKKO MOILANEN, MARJUKKA NIINIOJA, MARKO SEPPÄNEN, MIKA HONKANEN

API ECONOMY 101

Changes Your Business

First published in Finnish as *API-talous 101*, Alma Talent, 2018.

Cover & Layout: Marjukka Niinioja.

Translation: Marjukka Niinioja and other authors.

Publisher: BoD – Books on Demand, Helsinki, Finland

Printer: BoD – Books on Demand, Norderstedt, Germany

ISBN: 978-952-80-0849-1

Feedback about the book: *info@osaango.com*.

CONTENTS

PREFACE TO THE ENGLISH EDITION

After the Finnish edition was published in August 2018, we received so much encouraging feedback from our readers and requests from the people who couldn't read the book in Finnish to produce an English edition that we took the demand seriously. The task of translating the book from Finnish to English was quite difficult and costly because the languages are so different. We were grateful to get sponsors to help us use professional editing and allocate time from our busy schedules.

The companies and individuals who made this English edition possible:

Digia Finland Oy – leading digital software and service provider specializing in digital solutions, APIs, integrations and data services. Read more https://blog.digia.com/topic/api

Osaango Oy – API and platform economy educators, consultants and API developer experience reviewers. Osaango's APItalista and co-author of this book, Marjukka Niinioja created a free course related to this book with Tampere University professor Marko Seppänen, also a co-author. Join hundreds of others in the course at https://www.apieconomy.info
Foccus Design s.r.o. – providers of APItalks.com instant API for your data, based in Czech Republic, read more https://www.apitalks.com/

Heeros Oyj – makers of cloud-based financial systems provided in Finland and the Netherlands, read more:
https://www.heeros.com/en/

HH Partners Oy – attorneys at law focusing on technology, intellectual property and transactions, read more:
https://www.hhpartners.fi/en/

We would also like to thank companies and individuals who encouraged us to make this English edition come true, but who prefer to stay anonym. You know who you are dear family members, colleagues and ex-colleagues, business partners and fellow API-enthusiasts.
For the English edition to be possible at all, we'd like to give special thank you to Ari Nyfors from Transfluent for helping us get started with the project, to Erkki Saastamoinen and Sanna Toivanen from Kesko Oyj for all the worm support, Suna Koljonen and the whole Digia team for continuous support, fellow authors Amancio Bouza and Antti Merilehto for encouraging us both with their amazing attitudes but also sharing the good word on our book and Alena Vejsadová from Foccus Design for staying with the project all autumn and making it possible to get our book to the Czech audiences with a bang.

Helsinki, February 10th, 2019

Marjukka Niinioja, Marko Seppänen, Jarkko Moilanen and Mika Honkanen

PREFACE

The idea to write this book arose as Finland celebrated the 100th anniversary of its declaration of independence. We asked ourselves: How will Finland succeed in the next hundred years? How can we continue to ensure its competitiveness in the future? From the government's point of view, the platform economy and artificial intelligence play a crucial role; the intention is to be a pioneer in both.[1] Whether it is artificial intelligence or platforms, the application programming interface – i.e., the API – plays a key part in all this.

So why did we now decide to write the book? In short, the time is ripe and, according to our experience, the need to build (better) APIs and employ novel technologies in companies is great. In the global economy, Application Programming Interfaces have become an increasingly important way to produce applications, build ecosystems, and participate in the platform economy. To meet this need, we felt it necessary to create a resource aimed at business decision-makers, solution architects, and IT managers.

Our paths around API and platform economy issues crossed at many events and projects. In November 2017, at the initiative of Jarkko Moilanen, we put together our team of authors. Writing alone, the perspective would have been more limited and one-sided; together, we complement each other with our expertise and are able to offer our readers more diverse content.

Our main concern was to examine the development of APIs (often still in their infancy) being used by Finnish companies, how little APIs are understood as part of business models, and the competitiveness of organizations. Ecosystems are created with government funding and by encouragement, and there were hardly any examples of platform economy to speak of.

In Finland, APIs have entered public debate over the past couple of years. In August 2017, *Tivi* magazine wrote a comprehensive cover story titled "API Brings Money."[2] But do APIs and platform economy bring money to Finland, and if so, how will that happen? According to a study commissioned by the Finnish government, this is at least questionable.[3] A member of our author team, Marko Seppänen – together with a research team – has studied APIs and other platform economy boundary resources (explained in chapter 4) and their spread throughout the world. Finland is on the map in "good strokes," to use a sports term, but is not at the center of development.[4]

With APIs, the "circular economy" of the IT world changed shape. Prior to the extensive use of interfaces in service development, services were produced by recycling code. Code recycling has become more common with open source, and some of the best-known open source victors are the Linux operating system created by Linus Torvalds, the Apache web server, the MySQL database, and the Android operating system.

Open source code changed the world, and that change was based on code recycling and reuse.[5] The open source code is usually the basis for reference implementations[6] and co-developed platforms.

Since then, the development of applications and services has become API-based. With APIs, new product development reuses and recycles code, allowing programming interfaces to be productized – both yours and others'. Therefore, the openness of source code is not so central to API-based service development.

Exploiting the APIs of external organizations – often those outside of typical partnerships – in the development of a service contributes to the transformation of companies into ecosystems, because interdependencies are created between organizations. Switching to API-based service development will radically reduce development time. At the same time, the time-to-market for solutions is shortened. Speed is an asset and, therefore, API-based development has risen to default status.

From a business point of view, API facilitates rapid growth of the market for a company's products. Open APIs between companies, often referred to as partner APIs, open new digital routes for reaching end-users and provide consumers with new offerings. Instead of enduring a painful, months-long, traditional integration project, business collaboration can be done using APIs in weeks or even days.

Typically, partner interfaces are used to integrate a variety of services provided by several companies into ready-made packages. This, in turn, makes it easier for the end-customer to do business. The result is more service sales and a better customer experience; i.e., everyone wins.

Instead of a technical integration tool, APIs have started to become products in their own right or reusable tools for producing different applications.[7] Companies have therefore started to offer or sell interfaces on their own sites (so-called "developer centers") to their target groups. For these interfaces, the first forms of platform economy, such as common marketplaces, have been developed. One good example of this is Amazon Web Services (AWS).[8]

What happened to mobile applications has also happened to APIs, the only difference being the target group: mobile apps are sold to end-customers, and their installation and sales take place through consumer platforms (marketplaces) such as Google Play and Apple Store. "Platform" refers to a service and business model in which producers and consumers of a service or content meet and are partially overlapping. These appearances produce the desired network effect: the more consumers there are, the more service providers want to join the platform. This creates a loop that encourages both sides to produce more and more value for each other through the platform.

The APIs, in turn, are sold to the developers of these applications. However, the logic is the same: the product is introduced via the platform as a self-service product for either a fee or free of charge. Software developers became fascinated by the range of solutions available to speed up and facilitate the development of services. This interest gave birth to the API economy, where the API was no longer a byproduct or an additional feature accompanying the physical product, service, or information system. The API has increasingly become an independent, value-added product.

We hope this book will serve as a guide for your journey towards the API economy.

Tampere, April 30, 2018

Jarkko Moilanen, Marjukka Niinioja, Marko Seppänen, Mika Honkanen

SECTION I: BEGIN WITH BUSINESS

1 WARNING: THE API ECONOMY MAY CHANGE YOUR BUSINESS MODEL

Marjukka Niinioja

This chapter explains why business models are in transition and what is causing the change. We'll use examples to shed some light on how Application Programming Interfaces, or a lack of them, influence business models. In addition, we justify why interfaces[9] should also be on the agendas of businesses' decision-makers, not just on the IT departments'.

Think of a Book as an API and a Publisher as The Platform

Books have been printed since the 15th century, and since then, the publishing business has operated under the following simplified model: writers write, publishers publish and distribute, and both book publishers and bookstores sell.

Digitalization, the platform economy, and APIs have changed the business models and value streams associated with books. The change started with e-books and e-book reading devices. For example, book platforms such as lulu.com and BoD.fi, are built on their own APIs and those provided by other companies.

The "platform author" publishes his work for free as a self-published book. Through the platform, the book is distributed to domestic and international web and brick-and-mortar bookstores as an ebook or printed book. Books are printed automatically and only on request. Platform charges a commission per sold amount.

The platform offers added value: writers reap a larger share of the revenue and can decide on content and pricing, while readers enjoy a wider range of offerings and lower prices. Partners can publish series of books in a fully automated way. In general, the marketing of self-published books is largely based on search engines and the "long-tail phenomenon," wherein a niche-market product can be found online and acquire buyers even if it might be lost among traditional channels under bigger brands. The author's choice to self-publish a book or work with a publishing company does, of course, affect more than revenue. A prestigious publisher brings credibility to the book, as well as a skilled team and a well-tuned marketing machine. Self-publishing platforms work well if an interested publisher is not found, if the book is to serve as more of a marketing publication, or if the author has a readership that will find the book in any case.

The changes in the business model are significant – and enabled by APIs. The publishing platform typically utilizes other APIs, such as to create an ISBN and an EAN code for digital printing[10] and for publishing books on e-commerce platforms. In its most advanced form, it will be possible to offer the entire book via the API, predicts Hugh McGuire, founder of Pressbooks.[11]

"We Do Not Bother Business with This API Stuff"

API-related meetings in corporations are mostly private discussions on IT architecture and usually take place in the IT department. An API is the organization's own digital and sellable service product. On the other hand, it is also a commodity that can be bought. It can be a way to save money and time or improve the competence of the IT environment. It can also be a mandatory part of building a digital customer experience. All of these are related to a company's business model, which will define how value is created, shared, and combined using functions, resources, and competencies. There still exist numerous companies where the issue is briefly dismissed with, "We don't bother business with this API stuff." A visiting API consultant should be affixed with the label: "Warning – may change your business model."

For non-IT professionals, the API is initially a difficult technical issue to grasp, and it is surprisingly easy to confuse it with the "app," i.e., an application with a user interface installed (for example, on a mobile phone).[12] Technology is not the same as a business model, but technology has a significant impact on the feasibility of a business model.

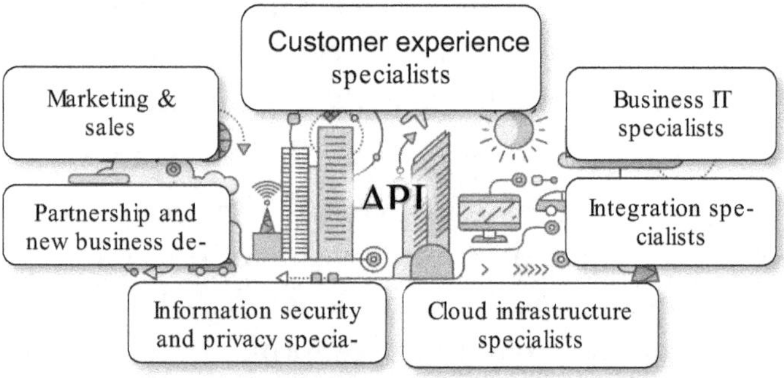

Figure 1 The entire "village" is needed for the API economy (all the functions necessary to buy, sell, and develop business-friendly, relevant, and safe APIs).

In addition to the publishing industry example presented earlier, this book introduces examples from the retail sector and its relation to APIs and the platform economy. We get to know Kesko (K Group), look at its competitor the S Group, and end up with a platform that offers Alibaba's interfaces, which is in fact so attractive that even Kesko has decided to join it.

With the help of Nordea and the Ministry of Transport, we are considering the impact of APIs on the banking and traffic sectors. We delve deep into the impact on business models and the operating conditions of companies within public sector-driven ecosystems and legislation requiring APIs. Will forced interaction produce new platform innovations and customer-orientation?

Currently, many companies are starting to resemble a technology enterprise. At the end of 2016, while working as Kesko's API Development Manager, Marjukka joked with a colleague, "When will Kesko management understand that it is leading a technology company instead of a retail and wholesale one?" (Then, a couple months later at the Paris retail fair, President and CEO Mikko Helander was asked the same question: whether he knows he's in charge of one of Europe's biggest technology companies.)

In late 2016, API development was just getting wind under its sails, partly supported by the fact that more digital services were being created than anyone could keep track of.[13] In the digital services for grocery trade, APIs had already been put into use. The business model and customer experience improvements for the building and technical trade's online stores were also being sped up by API development. The customer experience for homebuilders and renovators was greatly improved by not having to visit the stores' websites one-by-one when first trying to find a new sauna stove in stock, for example. APIs are used to calculate the distance from the customer's home to the store with the most stoves in stock or the particular model they are hoping to buy. The API even calculates the shipping costs using the data from the shipping agreements. The same APIs could also be used in the price signage and marketing displays of offline stores, digital marketing, and different digital channels, as well as via partners.[14]

API or Platform Economy?

The API can be part of the company's business model in many ways. It can be part of the company's offerings, or the company can exclusively sell APIs. An API can be a way of communicating with customers and partners or a way to improve the quality of information and reduce costs for a company's various internal services and systems. At its best, API can be a key element that attracts actors to the ecosystem and related platforms. In most cases of retailers and wholesalers, product manufacturers and other potential partners, especially large customers, are most interested in purchasing history and analysis.

What about order APIs? Whom should you provide access to orders via APIs? Is the channel and brand so valuable that it is not worth relying on others? Kesko and other Finnish retailers have thus far answered this question with a strong "maybe."

For example, in the autumn of 2017, the S Group announced that it would build an API layer.[15] The reasons for this were both the robustness of the current technical infrastructure (technical debt) and the construction of digital services, not so much to provide interfaces directly to partners or customers. However, in 2010, the S Group outsourced part of its platform and interface development to Digital Goodie (previously Digital Foodie), with whom it was collaborating.[16] So in 2016 the platform was sold to a US company.[17] Digital Goodie offers APIs, but information is only available to their partners (so there's no use looking for API documentation on the internet).

The market was caught by surprise for a moment in September 2017 when Kesko became a channel partner for Chinese Alibaba.[18] In this case, the Alibaba platform business model and its relatively well-marketed, publicly documented (compared to Digital Goodie) APIs were used. These APIs allow companies to place their products on the Alibaba online store platform.[19] Along with Amazon (operating a similar business model), Alibaba has grown into one of the largest online stores.

At the same time Finnish stores were facing challenges, especially online stores,[20] many foreign players have been able to create a comprehensive, fast-growing, and dynamic e-commerce, often thanks to the development of APIs and other user experiences that affect features for traders and suppliers. Of course, customizing the customer experience and simplifying the ordering process cannot be forgotten.

In a competitive situation, it is not always clear in which manner the business model should be changed or why. Often, companies have limited possibilities to influence their own models. The business is subject to restrictions or requirements that reduce the freedom of choice. Continuous price competition between all parties is shortsighted and drives companies into impossible situations. What if an operator from a completely different industry, with their particular platforms and a very different value proposal, were to suddenly appear and upset the market? What if the law changed so that a distinctive factor became mandatory for everyone? That is what happened, for example, in the banking sector with the PSD2 directive, when banks were forced to open their APIs to other players, and in Finland's transport sector, when the Finnish Ministry of Transport and Communications required the opening of ticketing APIs.

The Finnish Transport Agency presents the objectives of a project involving the opening of traffic-related APIs as follows: "With digitalization, mobility also changes to service (MaaS, Mobility as a Service). Mobility as a service is a very large ecosystem in which the travel chains handled as part of the 'interoperability of ticket and payment systems project ("LIPPU")' is one small but crucial part. From the customer point of view, the travel chain model helps journey planning and saves time. In the future, even more services, including ones other than mobility services, will be collected as service packages for customers. These packages will increase the appeal of services and will eventually bring more customers to all operators in the ecosystem."[21]

At this very moment, while writing this book, we will soon learn whether the transportation operators will really start selling each other's tickets or whether there will mostly be operators reselling tickets for different operators. What about customer experience and prices? In the Helsinki region, Whim – which connects different modes of transport to public taxis – has started operating at a fixed monthly price. Thus, operators in the transport sector must compete with applications that support their own brand and customer experience and deal with these intermediary services both as partners and competitors.

For example, Finland had a great app, Valopilkku ("BrightSpot"), for taxi services throughout the country. For a moment, however, the app was almost lost to competition because of new laws liberating the domestic taxi business. This change forced Finnish taxi providers to think about which ecosystems they wanted to operate within. At the time (November 2017), one of the biggest taxi operators, Taksi Helsinki, stopped using the Valopilkku app and developed their own. However, as Valopilkku offered a solution and an extensive nationwide network, Taksi Helsinki decided in May 2018 to buy the Valopilkku app for itself and continue its development. Obviously, where there are mobile applications, there are usually also APIs, and one might be able to also use them for other purposes, such as offering them to partners.

The common feature of "forced openings" for both the banking sector and the mobility interfaces is that the public sector decides to open the APIs but does not set clear guidelines for implementation. There are considerably more recommendations in the Finnish Transport Agency project than in the banking sector. Are these "free hands for developers" a good or a bad thing in the end?

Most of the interfaces of the banks operating in the Nordic countries are not particularly user-friendly. In other words, the developer experience[22] is poor and thus reduces the use of API and the attractiveness of the company in the partner network. Will the spirit of the PSD2 Directive be fulfilled if other companies are hesitant or unable to implement their own applications against poorly designed or documented interfaces?

As well, what is the significance of public-sector-defined API openings for businesses and their business models? For example, Nordea Bank has publicly stated that it views opening the APIs as a business opportunity, seeks to do it as well as possible, and as a result has contacted developer communities. We were thus interested in hearing more about how the Nordea API journey has progressed. Jarkko Turunen from Nordea answered us, saying, "Nordea's approach to PSD2 has been very proactive. Nordea opened its Open Banking portal for developers in spring 2017, after which over 1,600 developers have registered to test programming interfaces in the test environment. In the pilot phase, selected external service providers build applications on the interfaces and, together with the pilot customers, confirm that the Open Banking solution works in every respect reliably and as expected. The pilot will initially only use information from Finnish customers, after which customer information will also be included in other Nordic countries."

Turunen continued: "At Nordea, PSD2 is believed to offer opportunities for new business models where the bank and its customers and partners can benefit from new innovations and offerings. We are talking about the future payment and application ecosystems. In the future, API platforms will function as a new distribution channel for banking services. In addition to the mandatory PSD2 interfaces, Nordea sees the possibility of revenue streams in the Open Banking solution, for example through monetized Premium APIs."

In all the legislative and other changes widespread throughout the operating environment, there is usually a chance to turn the transformation into a competitive advantage for one's company. However, it may require joining the movement early, exceeding minimum requirements, and having courage. Also, in the banking sector internationally, various key players have prepared for the opening of APIs.

Open Banking is now on the lips of the international banking industry. It is not certain that the clients want Facebook, for example, to know the balance of their bank account, but this can be only a prelude. Legislation can also prevent the opening of interfaces or their use between different actors. An open dialogue between the public and private sectors is a necessity to secure business opportunities.

The most recent examples at the time of writing were the Canadian banks' demand not to cause unnecessary security threats amidst the PSD2 hype by requiring open interfaces and, on the other hand, the fact that due to legislation, banks cannot cooperate with fintech companies.[23] Banks are concerned about the distortion of competition, because fintech startups can turn to private investment companies with their product development ideas, unlike banks.

Summary

API technology affects business models.

An entire company's participation is needed to properly manage APIs.

APIs enable interaction with platform economy operators.

One's business model may encounter a "forced opening" of APIs at any time – see it as an opportunity.

If one's competitor offers (or is forced to provide) APIs, having the best developer experience is a significant competitive factor.

The API economy is not just part of platform economy, but APIs can be used for increasing internal productivity or for offering different business models.

2 WHAT VALUE DOES YOUR API ADD?

Marko Seppänen

This chapter discusses what is meant by an API's "added value" and why one should consider diverse ways to create it. In addition, consideration is given to how the API should be designed from the point of view of adding value. An API can add value to the application developers using it and to consumers of applications and devices containing APIs.

One particular company that provides contact information of businesses, individuals, decision-makers, and company risk classification information originally developed their API based on file-based integrations; the API was created mainly to meet the needs of large companies. The company received a lot of questions from the customer and partner developers when they tried to deploy solutions using the API. The deployments took several weeks on average. The company felt that using the API should be easier. Often, the API contained a lot of special vocabulary and classifications and often much unnecessary and detailed data in relation to the user's needs. The documentation was presented in PDF files and spread across several pages.

The company launched a project to improve the developer experience of the API. But what is easier and for whom, that is the problem. In the early stages of the project, Marjukka Niinioja asked if the project team knew for whom they were planning the upgraded API, as well as what customer journey the API should support. In other words, what added value and for whom should the API produce? This was not obvious at first, but with a short workshop employing appropriate methods, it became clear that the target group might even be the smaller companies. The most interesting target segment were those e-commerce entrepreneurs who needed to check their customers' risk classification and contact information before delivering more expensive purchases.

But do e-commerce entrepreneurs understand the API and how it can help them? And are they able to program, or do they have programmers in-house? In most cases, the answer is "no." They typically use a ready-made e-commerce platform or buy outsourced technical maintenance. So, are they the right target segment for the API? Would a simple API bring added value, even if it enabled an easier customer journey and less financial credit loss? Marketing the API to individual online merchants would probably be time-consuming and expensive. In addition, there will always be the issue of who integrates API into the e-commerce implementation. In addition to implementing their API, the real added value would only come from either implementing productized integration plugins into various e-commerce platforms or, even better, by designing and marketing the API to meet the needs of e-commerce platform vendors.

Added Value Is Experience

What, then, is the added value? There are different definitions of added value in economics, depending on whether we look at productivity or, for example, a company's profitability from the owner's (or investor's) perspective. In layman's terms, added value means the value experienced by the customer.

What, then, is the benefit? Traditionally, we are used to thinking about the benefits very concretely: I get more stuff, service, money, or anything else I want. The added value and the basis for the selection is that I carry out an intuitive comparison between the various options and select the service that I expect to offer the biggest benefits. Luckily, many other things that are not measurable in terms of money have also recently been understood as important factors in the selection process. We likewise – or even more so – appreciate the ease, speed, and even the image that the choice brings about. Such value factors have been highlighted in recent years, and companies are striving to improve their distinction by developing apt slogans and interesting brands.

On the other hand, the value experienced by the customer is structured in time before the acquisition, at the time of the acquisition, after the purchase, and at the time of withdrawal. This is described in more detail in the accompanying figure.

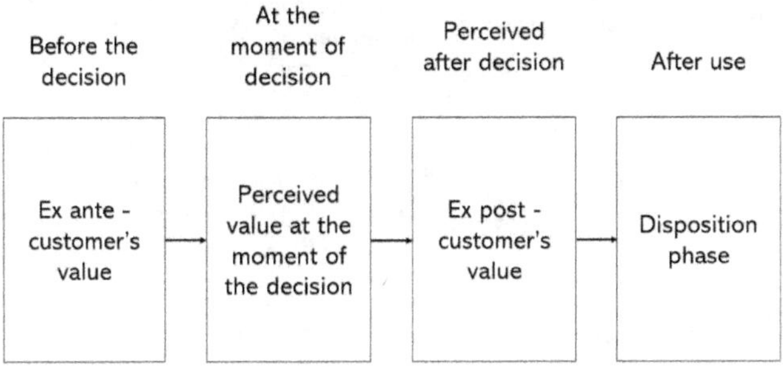

Figure 2 Value experienced in the acquisition process[24]

What are the components of the value at the various stages? We can divide it into five sections:

1. The difference between benefits and sacrifices (the "net value") 2. The sum of usage and experience 3. The value measured in monetary terms 4. The benchmark against others and 5. The value of discernible product properties

All these areas are always innately present, whether we are aware of them or not. From the customer's point of view, the interpretation of the perceived value may be different from that of the supplier of the product or service: if the value perceived and offered does not adequately satisfy, the trade does not occur. On the other hand, too high a price means that the customer perceives the product's or service's value – as compared to other similar products or services – to be disproportionate. Simultaneously, the same product or service may be more user-friendly and perhaps requires less learning and time. In this case, the benefits are more comprehensively balanced.

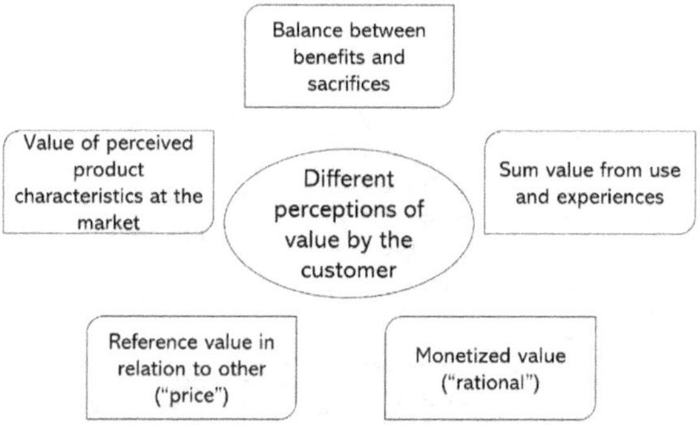

Figure 3 The value a customer experiences offers many different perspectives of interpretation. These service providers should be identified and approved[25]

Pieces of Added Value

The benefits and sacrifices described above can be broken into even smaller parts. Benefits can be viewed as features related to the product or service (for example, quality or customization). On the other hand, the use of a product or service results in different types of benefits for the customer, such as strategic benefit (e.g., an API gives a brand an image as a pioneer) or practical benefit (e.g., an API handles the standardization problem of a specific communication need).

Sacrifices can also be divided into monetary and non-monetary sacrifices. As a financial sacrifice, everyone easily recognizes the price, but the cumbersome tasks of acquiring the API product are costly. A well-designed and documented API reduces many of these expected costs. In addition, non-monetary costs are often overestimated; for example, using one's own time and the stress caused by difficulties in usage. These are all their own kinds of sacrifices that should not be overlooked. Often, only immediate and monetary costs will be considered, while many more depicted in the figure will be overshadowed. Making these factors visible can be crucial to securing a deal.

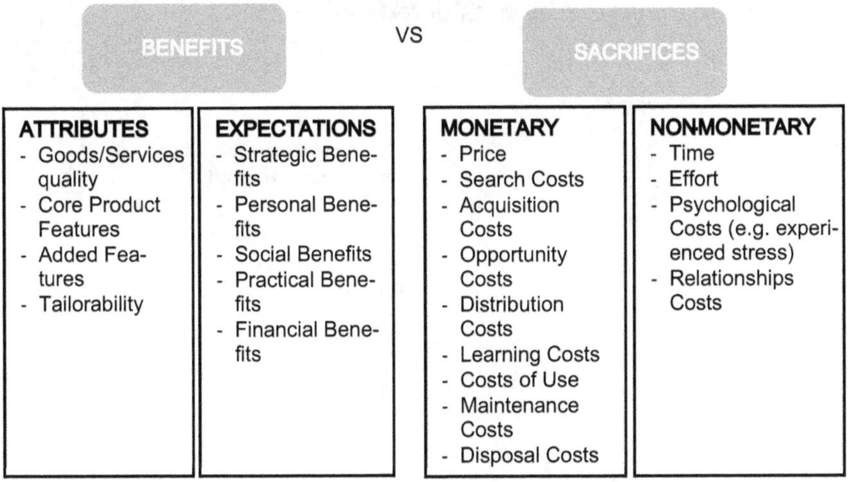
BENEFITS
VS
SACRIFICES
ATTRIBUTES
- Goods/Services quality
- Core Product Features
- Added Features
- Tailorability
EXPECTATIONS
- Strategic Benefits
- Personal Benefits
- Social Benefits
- Practical Benefits
- Financial Benefits
MONETARY
- Price
- Search Costs
- Acquisition Costs
- Opportunity Costs
- Distribution Costs
- Learning Costs
- Costs of Use
- Maintenance Costs
- Disposal Costs
NONMONETARY
- Time
- Effort
- Psychological Costs (e.g. experienced stress)
- Relationships Costs

Figure 4 Value consists of balance of benefits and sacrifices (modified from Woodall, 2003) [26]

When planning the building of an API, one should consider another more conceptual division: expectations between the API service provider and the user do not always meet, but a situation with the API or a variety of APIs may arise, as shown in the accompanying figure.

The provider can build in some customer value that the current customer does not need (so-called "unwanted value") and, on the other hand, some features ("non-delivered") that may not be delivered at all. The reason for such a problem boils down to communication: the parties may not have properly conveyed their own expectations and hopes to each other. On the other hand, if the parties are organizations, the reason may also be the so-called "broken phone" problem or even a lack of knowledge.

Sometimes, this imbalance is sought: the service provider has made strategic choices and sticks with them. Completely fulfilling the customization wishes of a single customer is rarely commercially feasible, and on the other hand – in addition to the needs of existing customers – parts of the offer may have been built to meet the needs of new customers. In such a rare case, the "negative" experience of an individual customer can be considered deliberate.

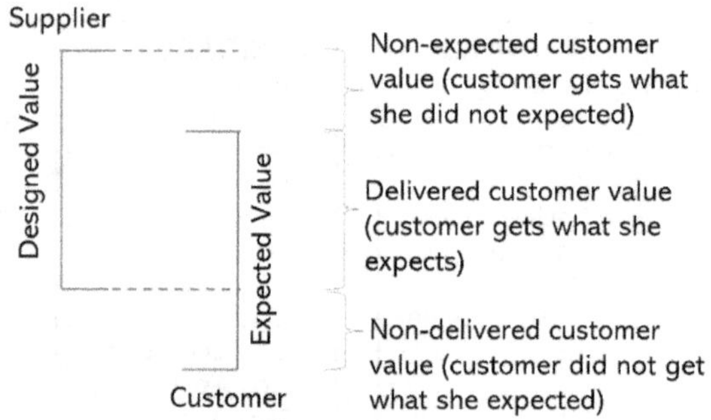

Figure 5 Implications of expected and received customer value[27]

This mechanism can be disassembled in more detail and linked to the previous emergence of benefits and sacrifices as shown in the figure below.

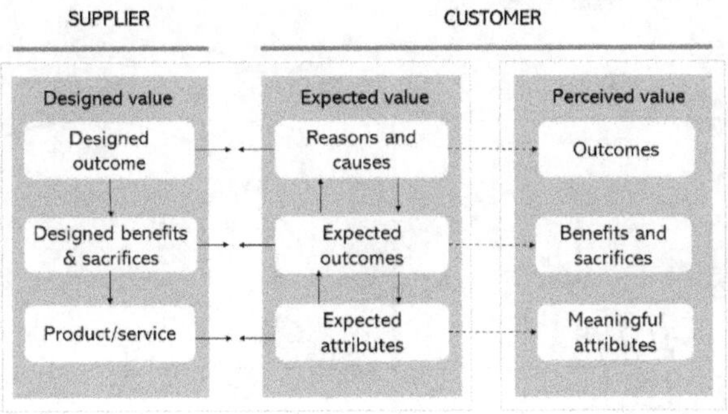

Figure 6 The multi-generality of value creation: the value the service provider means to the value the customer perceives[27]

API as a Means to Value

How does one slice value creation, and how can these fine slices be utilized in developing the organization's API products and services? The value proposition is at the heart of the business model (see chapter 12 for more details), and it is particularly important for the value proposition to build a summary that is the most suitable and easily understandable for the customer. The customer is supposed to either knowingly or unconsciously get something done, to do a job ("customer jobs"). Often, the definition of this need is made explicitly to provide a service or product as a solution to the need that the customer is supposed to have. A useful tool for defining the need may be, for example, the Value Proposition Canvas, by which the customer's[28] expectations of "pains" and "gains" can be linked to the parts of one's own offering ("pain relievers" and "gain creators"). Such a more detailed review is quite useful and often helps to overcome the gaps between expectations and realities as described above.

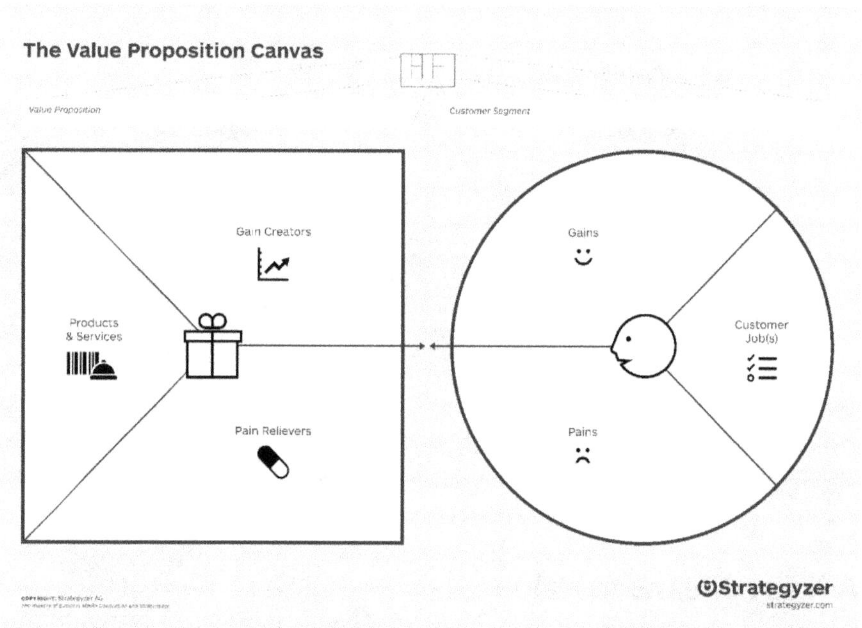

Figure 7 The Value Proposition Canvas is a means of structuring a customer's need and formulating a product or service concept to meet that need[29]

The API has five value-creating properties:[30] 1. The API reduces the complexity experienced by standardizing the implementation of the tasks. 2. The API provides better access to information or data by providing open (or limited, depending on desired choices) availability. 3. The API increases the chances of influencing content development by bringing new channel for data to providers and, on the other hand, users' needs are reflected in API's demand. 4. The API reduces the perceived risk because the dependence on a single API is small, and on the other hand the API is interchangeable with another with a relatively minor effort. 5. The API enhances the visibility of the service, encourages open innovation, and illustrates the benefits of an open data policy.

To sum up the main point: The API is an interface for capturing the value proposition, not just an interface for the application.[31] An

API can be a product itself or part of a larger entity. At the heart of everything, however, is the creation of value. One cannot predict a long lifespan for the API unless it is able to provide a noticeable and measurable value to any party.

Summary

Added value means the value experienced by the customer.

Experiencing value is multidimensional and consists of a wide variety of benefits and sacrifices.

API is one of the tools for generating business value, and an API can be a product in itself or an enabling factor as part of the customer's own value creation.

The value proposition tool should be used to concretize the value of the API.

3 APIS IN THE ECOSYSTEM

Jarkko Moilanen and Marko Seppänen

The chapter discusses the role of APIs in building a digital ecosystem. What are the benefits of an ecosystem? How does the ecosystem differ from the platform? How are API Economy and Platform Economy interrelated, and what is happening in the global API world?

Many of us have enjoyed skiing on the slopes of Lapland, camping in huts while enjoying pancakes, or watching the Northern Lights in a glass-roofed igloo. The same experiences are desired by more and more travelers outside Finland.

One of our authors, Jarkko Moilanen, has been involved in the creation of an ecosystem while working as an API economy consultant. One of the main tenets of the ecosystem is "Fell-Lapland as a platform," also known as the "Vamos!" ecosystem. The idea of the Vamos! ecosystem came from the need for business promotion. In this ecosystem, the various providers of experience services in Fell-Lapland, such as Ylläs, understood the point and initiated the creation of a new ecosystem with Finland's VTT Technical Research Centre.

An increasingly large share of the income from tourism in Fell-Lapland now comes from Asia. In order to get the experience on offer, the traveler needs to obtain airfare, solve transportation from the airport to the hotel, and get from the hotel to the slopes or to the ideal spot to watch the Northern Lights. Moving and traveling to destinations was unanimously seen as a compulsory evil. Instead of looking for and acquiring all the services from online stores of different service providers, it was decided to establish an ecosystem uniting key stakeholders in the Fell-Lapland region. The ecosystem operates on a common platform through which third parties – such as travel agents – can assemble experience packages with trips, using appropriate and well-designed APIs. The result is MaaS (Mobility as a Service) on steroids. Moving locally is handled by shuttle buses, locally rented cars, and shared taxis. Together with Finnair and VR (the national railway), an unbroken and versatile travel chain can be formed to help travelers better enjoy experiences.

The goal of the Vamos! ecosystem is to build a platform based on APIs. The platform is currently more of an API directory combined with API management. The parties' APIs can be found and deployed in one place. No stakeholder occupies the role of a gatekeeper but is accompanied by a neutral partner (VTT), which coordinates the ecosystem and ecosystem development. At the same time, each party is responsible for developing its own APIs.

Ecosystems are a New Cornerstone of Digital Business

Over the past couple of years, ecosystems have emerged in a number of discussions in both the public and private sectors. Ecosystems are seen everywhere – some are real, and some are mere hype without actual chances of success. There are innovation ecosystems, industrial ecosystems, and marketing ecosystems. A network is not the same as an ecosystem, especially when it comes to business. Operators in the same network have different types of connections ("structural holes") with each other.

Ecosystem operators, on the other hand, do not have similar connections but a common goal: *the ecosystem together generates value for its end-customers by integrating functionally interdependent subsystems.*[32] In this book, we focus on business ecosystems for which Ron Adner (2017) has provided a useful and recent definition:[33]

" An ecosystem is made up of a multilayered group of partners, all of whom and their interactions are needed to materialize a key ecosystem value proposition."

Ecosystems create "buzz" by bringing together several actors and producers. Operating in an ecosystem requires the adoption of a new philosophy of thinking and action. Instead of building our own silos, we should gather together to reflect on – and innovate – how to create a common and open ecosystem that is easy for everyone who wants to join. One of the exemplary sectoral ecosystems is the *software ecosystem*[34], which is a group of actors with a common market for their software and services, as well as interconnections. These connections are most often realized through a common technological platform and its APIs to exchange information, data, and resources. Recently, research has focused on identifying the health of such software ecosystems: How do we know the ecosystem is vibrant?[35] The same question and its answer is very important for any ecosystem and also for an organization thinking about joining the ecosystem.

In a platform-based ecosystem, the dominant operator is the platform owner, who coordinates and develops resources, providing them with tools for collaborative value creation.[36] Digital platforms are not just software platforms for collecting data but rather management systems that control, interact with, and refine data from value. This means that business development is more and more becoming an opportunity to enable social interaction in business – and this is done through digital platforms.[37] APIs are one of the key tools for crossing interfaces. More detailed information on platform-based business is provided in chapter 4.

Shared interests drive operators together. The so-called "red ocean" strategy[38], which is competing with the same products with similar features – thus leading to direct price competition – does not work. In contrast, the "blue ocean" strategy is looking for a new place on the market where there is no competition yet or creating a product that does not allow its competitors to respond.

In ecosystems, not all value is meant to be tied to your own company or product. Instead, solutions (APIs) from other ecosystem operators are utilized as part of product. The partners within an ecosystem create and cultivate a market collectively, allowing for value creation and the well-being and success of others, too. The idea is that the more potential customers there are, the more sales will be made. No one will necessarily find the desired and sought-after "unicorn" (i.e., a billion-dollar business), but common creation of opportunities will result in more sales than anyone could muster alone when engaged in bloody competition against others. It is not impossible that those who draw customers from the same market cooperate with each other.

APIs as Global Gateways

The API economy ecosystem differs from the traditional platform ecosystem in terms of governance. In the API economy ecosystem, new services are constantly being created by different companies and as mashups of APIs. If the use of an API becomes expensive or otherwise inappropriate, there is a very low threshold for switching to another API.

As digital services, APIs are accessible globally via the internet. The location of the companies that own them around the world is one way to perceive where development is taking place. API companies seem to be quite concentrated in a few urban areas, and most of the world is still at the same point – one could say at the starting point. The leading API centers are Silicon Valley (largely influenced by Google), Seattle (Amazon), London, and Washington, DC.[39]

Another way to perceive the API economy is to look at where these interfaces are used. This can be done by classifying the APIs and visualizing the size of the clusters formed and the relationships between them. We can notice that in some fields, such as e-commerce, mobile technology, and social media, APIs have gathered together. Thus, the API economy can be structured as shown in the accompanying figure. Noteworthy is that in 2015, banking and payment services were at the periphery of the API economy. It is assumed that the significant changes underway, such as ones posed by PSD2, will shift the focus of this review soon.

API subcategories' ecosystem has been studied and visualized.[40] This research shows how the APIs in different industries are and are not related to each other. API distributions by industry: social media and entertainment (29.6 percent); business applications and telecommunications (24.4%); search engines and databases (22.9%); data, analytics, and security (12.6%); and financial services and trade (10.4%). A significant part of the APIs in different industries are separate, so it is likely that overlapping development work has been done by developing separate solutions for the same need.

The third way to perceive the API economy is to review the API catalogs. The diversity of the API economy ecosystem can be seen by looking at the API catalogs the market has spawned, such as ProgrammableWeb[41] (over 20,000 APIs), APIs.io[42] (over 1,100 APIs), RapidAPI[43] (over 7,500 APIs), and APIs.guru Open API directory[44]. API catalogs partially contain the same APIs and act as a marketing channel.[45]

In short, in the ecosystem of the API economy, the focus is on the APIs instead of the platform. This enables a new kind of value creation with external partners, competitors, and various network communities and customers. There are many platforms in the ecosystem of the API economy, and the APIs on those platforms are consumed as part of service development. The API economy occurs at the outer edges and between the platforms, as illustrated below.

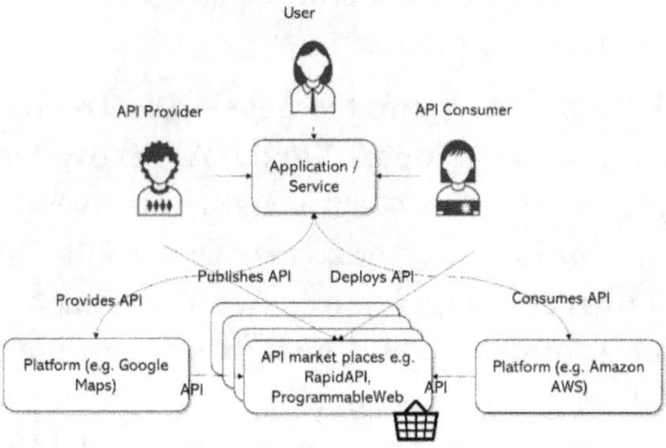

Figure 8 The API economy takes place between and around platforms.

The API economy ecosystem is currently displayed mainly in API catalogs. In principle, an API catalog can be thought of as a precursor to platforms whose main goal is to act as API marketplaces, offering benefits other than just visibility to API owners. An example of a simple API catalog is the first one, ProgrammableWeb, created by John Musser in 2005. In addition to the API listings, the service includes news, analyses, and reviews. In addition, they offer material curated by API University.

It is likely that API catalogs will contain the same features in the future as API management solutions. In this case, a business layer, billing functions, analytics services, and features for creating a developer experience are added to the API catalog using standard-based automated functions. This trend is represented by, among other things, the RapidAPI service, which already provides some of the above services to API providers. RapidAPI not only adds value to API owners but also provides APIs to service users, at a glance, to see the status of the APIs they use and to easily find and deploy new interfaces. By generating added value for developers, traction towards consumers (API users) is created and at the same time, the size of the target audience grows, thus attracting more API providers. Therefore, we can say that API catalogs and marketplaces will continue to be platforms among other platforms.

In the platform ecosystem, the developers are more at the mercy of the platform owner compared to the API ecosystem. On the other hand, the global API ecosystem consists of several multipart platforms, because it is characterized by less control of the platform owner, multiplayer competition between common consumer markets, free price formation, and interaction with the other players.[46] This arena of competition is developing at a brisk pace, and Finnish players especially have to consider the playing field as truly global.

Summary

Different ecosystems have been a topic of discussion in Finland in recent years. Building a successful ecosystem requires innovative architecture to provide access to knowledge, to participate in standardization, and to invest in the creation of complementary components and services. Usually, the platform owner is responsible for these.[47]

One question worth considering is the classic chicken-or-the-egg problem: Does the ecosystem build itself around APIs, or do APIs arise from the ecosystem? One can reasonably say both are potential routes. It seems that, in most cases, APIs themselves are not necessarily enough to build ecosystems, but rather the value creation (value proposition) of an ecosystem requires the existence of certain types of complementary components. Put simply, the value creation of an ecosystem requires that APIs bring their own added value to the whole.

APIs are the key to building and constructing digital ecosystems in their present form. APIs are a new type of enabling resource that can be used flexibly and in diverse ways to create new kinds of offerings. Thus, the API catalogs created to identify and search for suitable APIs are tools for bringing APIs together as marketplaces or modern virtual bazaars.

4 TRACTION IN THE PLATFORM ACTION

Marko Seppänen

The platforms and the business based on them, the so-called "platform economy," is one of the most significant long-term changes underway. After the service-oriented thinking of the 20th century, as well as of the last couple of decades, the next big disruption is taking place within platforms. The purpose of this chapter is to shed light on this turmoil and its effects.

Value Comes from Interaction

William Gibson allegedly said, *"The future is already here – it's just unevenly distributed."* This statement also applies to the platform economy: so-called "GAFA companies" (Google, Apple, Facebook, and Amazon) are well-known examples of how the nature of business has already changed in many areas. These gigantic new businesses are reforming value creation and especially the distribution of profits, exceeding the boundaries of different industries. For example, Apple's cash reserves are many times larger than the annual budget of the Finnish state. With such resources, it is possible to carry out massive and rapid development work.

Interaction requires that the platform attracts, engages, and connects both value providers and users. Value and participants, both users and producers, form the core of the platform: core interaction.[48] Interaction begins with the co-creation of value with users and producers, and often the platform uses so-called "filters" in the common creation of value. Based on the algorithm's recommendations, the digital platform automatically provides the user with the services best suited to their needs. Recommendations can be based on, for example, the customer's purchase history or by combining information from similar purchases by other customers. The algorithms thus create value between producers and users.

By understanding the core interaction and the value to be exchanged, it is easier to define the key enablers for the network effects. For example, using a phone requires a direct network effect: the more friends it can maintain within its network, the more value the phone poses to the user. Owning a single telephone, as such, does not bring value unless it has antique or other aesthetic or cultural value. Similarly, an example of an indirect network effect is Facebook: the more we produce content and spend time with content produced by other users (and service providers), the more valuable the Facebook application is to the customer, platform, and its suppliers. Ads are also called third-party content, and they still produce most of Facebook's revenue.

The platform provides the infrastructure and rules for a marketplace that brings together producers (suppliers) and users (customers). The ecosystem operators have four principled roles:[49] platform owners, service providers, suppliers, and customers. The roles can also change rapidly on the same platform or coexist (i.e., "common value creation," where the customer participates in the value creation of the service together with the supplier).

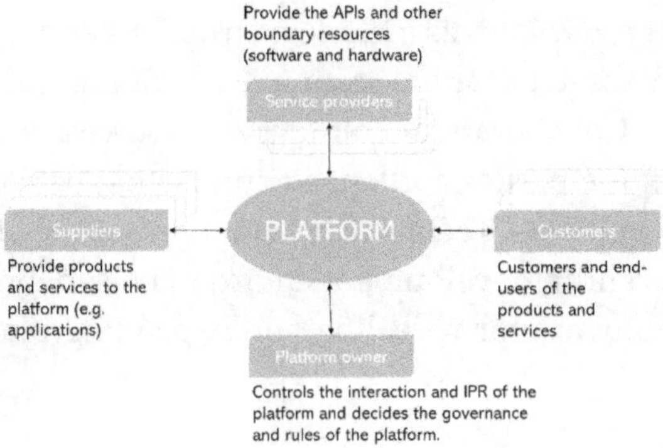
Provide the APIs and other boundary resources (software and hardware)
Service providers
Suppliers
PLATFORM
Customers
Provide products and services to the platform (e.g. applications)
Customers and end-users of the products and services
Platform owner
Controls the interaction and IPR of the platform and decides the governance and rules of the platform.

Figure 9 The basic roles of the platform operators

A key technological resource is the platform itself, which may be, for example, software, system architecture, or even a protocol. From a technological point of view, a technical platform may be an independent software or desktop application; equally, however, it may be other software or services, such as Google Maps or Eclipse. APIs are increasingly becoming part of the technical boundary resources of platforms for different ecosystems.

Boundary resources are determined by the chief stakeholder, the one who bears the greatest influence.[50] The purpose of boundary resources is to enable the stakeholder's ability to control and influence what is happening in the ecosystem while at the same time taking advantage of the work of third-party developers. In addition, the boundary resources are used to minimize the need for coordination between the third-party developers and chief stakeholder. These developers are often developer or user communities, which are further described in chapters 10 and 16.

There are two types of boundary resources: collaborative and technical. Collaborative boundary resources are, in practice, agreements and guidelines between the platform owner and the service provider attached to it. These resources include instructions and manuals, documentation, intangible capital contracts, training materials, and online forums. Collaborative boundary resources transfer information between the parties and enable interaction between the platform and the developers. Technical boundary resources, for example, are APIs, SDKs, entire development environments, debugging tools, and compiler software for revealing and expanding platform architecture.

Why do business models change?

The platform economy[51] is a recent phenomenon that forces former production- and service-centric organizations to think about and develop new methods. At the same time, business models have to be largely redesigned. Instead of ownership and exchange of ownership, interaction is becoming the foundation of business. The interaction between many parties requires new courses of action, both technically and cooperatively. Technically, one specific and useful interactor is the API. In addition, the central role in the creation of interaction is the trust between the parties. Rachel Botsman[52] has summed up this evolving scenario by saying that confidence is "the new money" – the new economic tool for the new economy.

Traditionally, trust has existed locally, between individuals. For hundreds of years, societies have held institutional confidence – trust – in the guidance and knowledge provided by churches or universities, for example. Technological advancement undermines this institutional confidence. Today, for example, every citizen can tweet as easily as the Pope or a professor. Valuation and credibility of a single tweet and its reach is evaluated by various algorithms. It remains to be seen to what extent institutions can innovate and adapt to this development. Or is there an unprecedented period of individualism geared to be the next step for us? In terms of platform economy, what is important in this development is that the mechanisms for recommending the services provided by the platforms are suitable and flexible to support such an era of trust. On the other hand, consumer confidence is volatile, and not even companies are shielded from the deterioration of institutionalism; a corporation can easily lose one's trust.

The principles of platform economy are as follows:[53]

- The platform provides its consumers with external resources. For example, Uber does not own cars or hire drivers.
- Creating rules and managing and improving interaction between consumers and producers is one of the platform's key tasks. Interactions *are* the core content of the platform.
- Value is created through novel combinations of existing resources, ideas, and business models.
- Resources can be those that may otherwise be unused (for example, sofas and guest rooms offered through Airbnb).
- The platform that improves the interaction between consumers and producers is the most successful, because it creates the most value. The winning platform is simultaneously orchestrated in terms of efficiency, development, and innovation and can simultaneously be internal, open, closed, and leading.[54]
- On the platform, consumers often also become producers (e.g., a platform for recycled goods like OLX Group[55] where consumers sell their own goods).

In practice, platform economy means; for example, the creation of a world of value-added services around a physical product such as a mobile phone. In addition to its mobile phones, computers, and iPads, Apple also has a store (App Store) for downloading various applications and content to devices. Apple offers a set of tools and rules for developers to ensure interoperability and compatibility with their platform. Anyone can develop their own content on this platform, but

Apple controls access to the site and charges 30% for use of the platform. This Apple platform has been used by, for example, Supercell, whose games are sold around the world.

Another platform where Supercell games are sold is Google Play, which has a similar business strategy. In principle, the platform is open to everyone, but Google takes its share of the use of its ecosystem and determines the conditions under which others can use the platform. It is noteworthy that everything at Google is built on APIs, including Gmail.

API Economy: A Platform Economy Forerunner

According to an article in Forbes, 2017 was the year of the API economy.[56] In an API economy, a company can sell content, services, terminal or invoice logic, or even physical resources through an interface, API. The API can thus be an independent product, can be sold on the marketplace (on its own or through someone else's platform), or it can be an integral part of the physical product. An API can also simply be a tool for making more efficient use of internal or partner resources to produce its own services or products.

In addition to platforms, APIs are used for:

- Orchestration of business models, open business models, and innovations
- Informational products and predictive and cognitive intelligent services
- Building multi-channel services
- Personalization of services and knowledge

In Finland, there is still a very small platform economy[57] based on digital platforms and the API economy compared to some other countries, significantly weakening its international competitiveness. Why is that so? Because the platform economy seems to be related to the "winner takes all" phenomenon. In other words, the company that secures the winning platform will reap the biggest profits. The development has mainly been driven by the US-based GAFA companies, but there are also significant players in Asia. From this point of view, too much emphasis cannot be placed on the value of big and wide data at the heart of value creation. The collection of data requires specific expertise, as does as its processing; for example, machine learning and deep learning.[58] It is hardly an exaggeration to say that data refineries will replace oil refineries in the future as a source of national wealth. The development and application of artificial intelligence in the business of digital platform companies has resulted in Baidu ("China's Google") and Tencent becoming important actors alongside Alibaba.[59] Extensive and multidimensional data masses utilized in the development of artificial intelligence algorithms offer opportunities for significant competitive advantage.

In order to improve Finland's competitiveness in the public sector, several projects have been launched in recent years to develop platform and API skills. In addition, the EU has contributed to the development of APIs by means of directives, but at the same time a major shift has taken place, among other places, in the banking sector. These projects do not eliminate companies' responsibility for developing business models; on the contrary, they require a more innovative and determined development of business models, where APIs and the platform economy play a major role.

Summary

The platform economy is a new operating model, which rolls back both industry boundaries and companies' profit-distribution models. The API is one of the key boundary resources, and it enables a new kind of value creation in the platform economy. The role of large multinational companies, including the GAFA companies, are and will continue to be massive in the future. In addition to the development of technology and services, trust in the platform economy is growing, both between individuals and institutions. Transparent development of artificial intelligence and algorithms can be one of the necessary means for maintaining and building that trust.

We asked Mikko Dufva (Sitra), Heidi Auvis (VTT), and Raija Koivisto (VTT) to open the doors to the future of the platforms:

Trends in Platform Economy

The debate on platform economy has shifted from pondering the interfaces of technology platforms to perceiving new business models and opportunities and, more recently, calling for social impacts and rules of the game. At the same time, there are signs of change in the way relatively centralized platform companies move towards a more decentralized network and business ecosystem. Rising technologies such as the block chain, Internet of Things (IoT), and artificial intelligence create new opportunities for platforms. In order to understand the platform economy, one has to look at the combined effects of technologies and the prevailing perceptions of the platform economy.

In the Platform Value Now project (platformvaluenow.org), we have summarized the recent changes in the platform economy as four general developments:

1) *A change in the amount and use of information:* Plenty of information is generated and produced in the operation of platforms. That information is increasingly also being analyzed, processed, or resold, in addition to being collected and stored. Data ownership is a topic of increasing debate, and the EU has a different stance on it than the US or China. Blockchain technology provides new tools for determining the ownership of information and allows for the intelligent retention of information. Artificial intelligence helps handle large data masses, but it has its own problems such as repetition of old biases and difficulties in understanding algorithms.

2) *Increasing environmental intelligence:* Platform economy has been significantly boosted by the proliferation of smartphones, which introduce platforms almost everywhere and track the location of the user. It seems that the evolution seems to be moving from smart phones to smart environments and the IoT. In addition to sensor and battery technology, new 5G networks are essential.

3) *Decentralization of value creation and value distribution:* In the platform economy, attention has been focused on value creation, and the discussion on the distribution of value has been overshadowed by platform monopolies. Recently, however, there have been examples of different ways of sharing value in platforms. The co-operative platform is owned by its users, and the decision-making power and the value created by the platform are then shared among the users. In turn, business models based on the block chain tend to eliminate human indeterminacy by fully interacting through conversion of contracts into code. However, the first experiments have shown that it is difficult to put everything in code, and some sort of interpersonal and dispute resolution mechanisms are needed.

4) Sluggish platform economy behavior models: At the moment, the discussion about the platform economy is dominated by the great promises of the new channels of value creation and, on the other hand, the threat of disruption in various industries. This model of domination and concentrated power leads to the image of the platform economy as a train that one must jump onto. Such an approach covers the idea of a platform economy as a form of interaction shaped by its users, of which behavioral patterns are only just being learned and shaped.

5 API – A PRODUCT, SERVICE, OR SOMETHING ELSE?

Marjukka Niinioja

This chapter discusses the different forms of API and their significance for business and technical development. The chapter also answers the question of what API is and what is its optimal role as part of a company's business model and IT architecture.

"API is a product. API is a product. Did I already mention that API is a product?" With these words, Jarkko Moilanen hypnotizes his audience at Digital Tampere in November 2017. Jarkko is talking to the developer community about being involved in the product development phase of an API. The "API is a product" message has been spread over several years by companies offering API management technologies and API consultants around the world. Yet, the large API audience has not yet internalized it, only seeing APIs as "a piece of code" and a method of integration.

The API-as-a-product paradigm takes our thoughts in a standardized, even commercialized direction. However, as we wrote this book, we noticed that we were questioning whether the product perspective is enough to describe the essence and use of the API. There are also several instances in which the API is an additional service as part of a physical product or in which an API actually provides a service provided by people or at least a continuous service that could have been previously provided human-to-human.

Some APIs provide information in either raw or processed format. In this case, one can discuss whether the API is itself:

- a product (compared with a book or a newspaper)
- a service (compared with a search service, professional service provided by an information specialist)
- technology (compared with email protocol SMTP / IMAP)
- a resource (for example a useful production resource, e.g., facilities, persons, machines or raw materials)

The whole API problem starts with the name, Application Programming Interface. There is usually at least a light application layer beneath the interface. It can be *very* light and can control or read, for example, a physical device and its sensors – and thus a great mass of information. For example, a minimal interface may have a static or permanent file that people will update if necessary.

However, seeing API as a software product does not lead to much. At least if O'Reilly (2007) is to be believed: "In the API era, software will never have to be shared but only performed. Interfaces are central to the information they handle, otherwise they are virtually useless. "[60]

"API Included"

From the shop, I buy a bulb for our living room ceiling light fixture. There are several different models and wattages to choose from, but the choice is also hampered by the API – or rather a lack of one. Do I want to control our living room lighting system with our home control system or maybe with a mini computer by writing my own script[61]?

However, with lighting one needs to be careful, as the systems often do not offer an API for public use: they can only be used with the remote control or directly from the device. I mistakenly purchased a LED strip with a different color for a work project and a light strip with no API but a USB connector. At first, I thought I could easily control the USB connector, but it wasn't that simple. The light strip ended up entertaining my teenage boy and his friends as a homemade disco light.

In any case, APIs have made their way into the home and office as well as yard and garden, but the API's world domination has gone unnoticed by a wider audience. For example, several robotic vacuum cleaners and lawn mowers have an API. In one of my workplaces, the CEO proudly brought the new posh coffee machine to the office. It used higher quality beans, and other great features were introduced to us. Alas, the team's first question was, "Is there an API?" After seeing the CEO's astonished look, we explained, "With an API, you can monitor the number of coffee beans, the machine's standby mode, and the temperature of the milk refrigerator at your workstation." The task could not have been achieved with a web camera, because it could have affected privacy. Well, there was no API in the boss's purchasing criteria, and the model containing API would have been a little more expensive. (It is advisable to make note of this important criterion when purchasing such a kitchen appliance.)

Of course, products containing an API are not made only for geeks to be able to program their home and office full of fun gadgets. From a television manufacturer's point of view, for example, it is generally advisable to provide an API by default, because the manufacturer or partners themselves can implement various control applications and devices, such as a mobile remote-control application. (It has saved the day for us many times when the universal remote can't be found.)

Seriously speaking, television, lamps, and robots could already be easily connected via APIs to the same or different manufacturers' home control systems. The ecosystem is ready without extensive product development and marketing efforts in specialized areas. So far, this has not been widely possible between devices from different manufacturers, but the situation is improving.[62]

APIs can also be found on larger machines and devices. For example, some car manufacturers[63] jumped into the API economy at an early stage, though not early enough for open APIs, at least according to their users[64]. Information security has not been the first requirement: hijacking a speeding car and opening doors with APIs has not really made customers smile. Tesla did not expressly consider its internal API to be used by car owners, and they weren't happy when it happened.[65] In addition to cars, APIs can be found in a paper mill production machine, bus, or elevator. An API is useful for device or vehicle status, its location, for assessing its maintenance needs, and to connect the device to an interoperable set of technologies from different manufacturers.

In the previous examples, we bought physical goods and the API came as a bonus. What if you buy an API to control your goods? For example, flying mini-helicopters or drones can be controlled using drone platforms. The IoT platforms offered by various manufacturers provide the ability to control or at least read almost any devices and sensors that can be connected by different techniques. These platforms are provided as either open or closed source code software libraries or cloud services. The platform can be deployed on your own device or installed in a ready-made cloud environment. Deployment and payment in the cloud take place according to usage or with a monthly fee. There are even several Finnish IoT platforms.[66]

At this point, we are already seeing a shift to the service dimension of APIs, where interfaces are offered as productized and standardized services. This change is also related to a broader product-oriented logic (PDL) for the transition to service-oriented logic (service-dominant logic, SDL).

Providing interfaces in productized and standardized environments is the theme of the day in many big organizations. Often, interfaces are implemented from the integration point of view – customer and system specific. Over time, they have been born in hundreds or even thousands. APIs and the underlying information, algorithms, devices, and other resources should be thought of more as services.

APIs can also be used to shift the sale of physical goods to service ("servitization"), meaning situations where a physical product, instead of buying and transferring ownership, can be offered as a rental or other service. For example, in the IT sector, we are seeing a transition from server ownership to the introduction of capacity and even higher-level services, such as software-as-a-service applications (SaaS) or machine learning solutions.

Cloud computing makes data processing capabilities and services easy with a few API calls. On the other hand, when not needed anymore, the abandonment of services and capacity will be easy with an API, and payments will be made only according to the time used. Previously, the only way to get your software running on a server was to contact an IT service provider by email and order an operating system, software licenses, additional disk space, or new physical server hardware and then installing everything.

Resource-oriented API Worldview

Companies need to make an inventory at regular intervals to know what and how many resources they have at their disposal. When a company moves into the API era, it must also make an inventory from the API perspective.

According to Richardson's definition[67], a resource is anything to refer to. You can create a hyperlink to it, retrieve or store its data, comment on it, or perform other operations related to it. A resource can be something that can be stored on a computer or at least referenced. It can therefore be a physical object (e.g., a car from which you can enter a character, serial number, registration number, drawings, ownership, and other information into your computer). It can also be an abstract concept, such as a feeling. However, according to Richardson, the resource is established through its unique link, a URI (Universal Resource Identifier), and only things with URIs exist on the internet.

Many software professionals are familiar with Fielding's dissertation[68], which introduces the basic principles of the RESTful web services architecture. Fielding's doctoral dissertation is one of the basics of the Internet and especially API. It is the first one to take a stand on how to design REST APIs. For Fielding, all internet services appear as resources.[69]

From a business point of view, an API is primarily a resource that can be sold and purchased like any other. Resources are indispensable for the business model to work, writes Marko Seppänen (one of the authors) in 2009[70]. Seppänen is in line with Richardson, although from a business perspective. According to Seppänen, resources must be identified and available. Identifying and evaluating all resources are important to find out what resources are already in use in the company and what is needed for new resources to implement the business model.

All this, of course, leads to the question of what exactly resources are. You can't identify what can't be categorized. In their research, Seppänen and Mäkinen[71] have found seven different types of company resources generally recognized by both researchers and leaders. Based on the results of this study, Marko Seppänen and Marjukka Ninioja developed a new model that describes the resources available to the company specifically in the API economy.

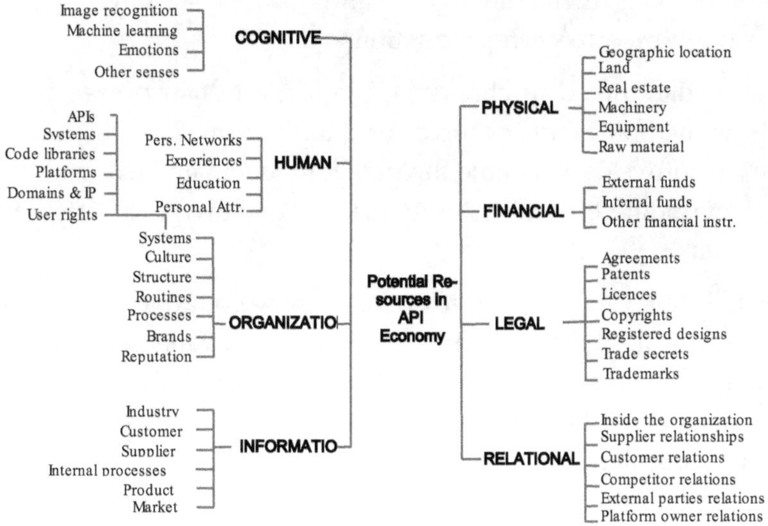

Figure 10 Business resources in the API economy (Marko Seppänen and Marjukka Niinioja)

If you are wondering what interfaces your company should develop and offer, at least internally, the above graphic can serve as a shopping or product development list. All the resources described in the model could and should be provided through APIs.

The most important resources of the platform economy company are knowledge and APIs related to the resources of other companies and organizations. It should be possible for others to offer complementary information about their own taxis, dwellings, premises, books, and websites via the APIs of the platform company.

Relational resources and human resources should have the necessary capabilities to identify, categorize, retrieve, and automatically improve the platform's customer experience and the optimal use of resources by operators. To complement human resources, a modern platform can utilize cognitive (i.e., human-like abilities) modeling resources based on artificial intelligence and machine learning, such as image recognition or speech production.

As previously noted in chapter 4, platform industry researchers see APIs as the boundary resources of the platform. The purpose of boundary resources is to enable the platform to join and exit and, for example, to update or read from its platform its own products, services, or data.

Seppälä[72] states that it is characteristic of these boundary resources, which are typically in digital form, that they are available freely (or for a small fee) on the internet for use by third parties. This definition corresponds well to the term "open" used by international APIs and technology suppliers. Open interfaces include "public" APIs and "partner" APIs. The designation depends on the relation of the interface user to the entity providing the API.

The following table compares the concepts of internal API, partner API, and public API. Thus, the internal API is not publicly available, its use is not charged for (unless the internal API is the API for the internal product) and its data is open to the organization but not necessarily to the entire organization. An open API should also be separate from an open data API, where API provides open access to information for others.[73] The next section discusses each concept more in-depth.

	Available for use	Support publicly available	Monetized	Open Data
Open Data API	Yes	Yes	Usually free at first, but as the requirements increase,	Yes, the license attached to the content defines the permissions

				there may be a charge.	
Open API	Public API	Yes	Yes	Often yes, although may include free tier.	Maybe
	Partner API	No	Yes	Not usually, included in the partnership.	No
Internal or Private API		No	No	No	No

Table 1 API Classification (Marjukka Niinioja and Jarkko Moilanen)

Not all open APIs are platform boundary resources. An open API can also be an independent service, such as a language translation algorithm or a specialized service for sending emails and other messages.

Summary

API is...	Description	Example	Type of API
Important feature of a tangible product	API is part of a tangible product or productized service. Customer gets the API as part of the deal when buying the product.	Internet of Things (IoT) APIs for controlling and analyzing state of things like home appliances or sensors	Partner or public, sometimes also private
Productized service	API in itself is a productized service, offered to all customers in the same way	Translation APIs, Payment APIs	Public API

Part of a digital or real-world service	API is part of the service experience, for example maintenance service is ordered with an API, or you can monitor package delivery with an API	Logistics API	Partner or Public API
Customer-specific service	API is part of a service offered to customers as a tailor-made solution including for example an integration to a service providers system.	APIs in customer specific applications	Partner
Interface to resources	API is just a means to access a resource the company is selling	Company info APIs (risk category, owners, contact information). Cognitive APIs etc.	Open data APIs, Partner APIs
Interface to platform (boundary resource)	API is a means to connect with a platform and get added value through participation in the interconnecting relationships of the platform (in Platform Economy business model)	Online auction API, Apartment sharing API	Partner or Public
Part of an integration	API is means to connect in to applications and devices	Product API, Employees API, business transactions API	Internal or partner API

Table 2 APIs can be categorized according to their user base and purpose. They can also be broken down according to their role in a company.

6 BUSINESS MODELS FROM APIS TO PLATFORMS

Marjukka Niinioja

This chapter explores options for business modeling in the API economy and how interfaces can be exploited with existing models. In addition, the chapter discusses the concept of a business model and, with examples, differentiates between traditional business models and API business models. The chapter also discusses how easily the API will transform the business model into a platform. The key angles of review for business models are growth potential, market size, and revenue and cost structure.

Business models make one think of money. Money can come to mind because of the lack of it or earning of it, but both involve payment. There are many well-designed and affordable payment-related examples among the business models of the API economy.

Stripe, one of the largest API-based payment brokers, has been in operation for over five years and has made $20 billion in revenue with payment transactions. This has been achieved in practice with safe and well-produced APIs. Who can say the same? Braintree was previously Stripe's only viable competitor in the international API-based payment market, but PayPal acquired Braintree in 2013 because PayPal's business model was no longer competitive enough.

PayPal's business model was primarily based on user interfaces and only interfaces with trusted partners. The monetization model was much more complicated: users had to pay for every feature separately. With the purchase of Braintree, PayPal was able to take on new business and pricing models. Braintree, in turn, was able to take advantage of PayPal's payment transfer network.

One of the key elements of the PayPal business model is to act as a "wallet" for the customer, where the customer can deposit money or different means of payment, if desired. The competitive situation in this business has been steadily increasing as more and more wallets are being added all the time. Payment methods have also changed. For example, the local payment and various payment applications on phones have changed the field substantially. With the help of API, Braintree has built a platform where merchants can integrate their required wallets without the need for programming.[74] The customer experience has also changed: because payments are delivered directly via API-enabled social media to suppliers of goods and services, the merchant's traditional online store may no longer be used.

Domestic operators providing payment APIs have arisen in recent years, including in Finland. Checkout Finland, calling itself Finland's largest payment provider company, was acquired by OP Financial Group. The Checkout Finland business model includes network-like activities, where different parties produce card payments and other services as part of their payment arrangements. Checkout Finland offers API and plugin-type interfaces for various e-commerce platforms.

The essential aspects of the business model are the target groups and the relationships and channels with which they are maintained. It seems that OP's strategy following the acquisition of Checkout Finland is to own several payment channels in connection with mobile payments and online payments and to facilitate the use of the network and mobile merchant service.[75] Checkout Finland's API can deliver payments through their service and network. In this respect, Checkout Finland and Stripe are similar in their business model, while Braintree leverages the platform business model and invites users to bring any payment providers' wallets into their service.

The table below includes a comparison of the above services at March 2018 rates. Price and service information are indicative. It is essential to see the differences in how complex services are priced and what features they include. However, the selling price is just one part of the business model or even the revenue generation. The volume and profitability of net sales are significantly affected by the cost structure and of course the volume and size of the market. It is quite different to build a network or think about solutions from the point of view of a single country than that of a global business.

Service	PayPal	Braintree	Stripe	Checkout Finland
Transaction fee	2.9% + 30 c	1.9% + 0.30€	1.4% + 0.25€ (Europe)	3% + 0.50€
With payment cards, billing from a web page	$30 / Month		Free	Free
Payment refund	$20 / piece	30 € / piece	$15 / piece	0,50 € / piece
Micropayments (under $10)	5 % + 0,05c		Included in fixed price	-
Refund	Fixed fee		Free	
International cards	1 %	+1 % in different currency 2,9 % + 30 c (AmEx)	2,9 % + 30 c	N/A
Card authorization	30 c		Free	N/A
Recurring billing	$10 / month		Free	N/A, PayPal can be used

				with their pricing
Fraud detection	$10 / month		Free	-
Apple Pay	-		Free	-

Other Critical Aspects of the Business Model

In the API economy, developer experience is a key part of customer experience and business model success. Stripe developer experience has long been legendary among developers, so good that it has even been a key success factor in addition to a clearer pricing model. Braintree believes in ready-made software development packages instead of offering API, while Stripe has a very clear REST API. Its API is also well designed, modern, reliable, convincingly documented, and easy to use. Checkout Finland's API is located at github.io. Although the documentation is comprehensive, it could be somewhat clearer for users who are new to the payment transfer business. This is discussed more extensively in chapter 10, but it should be noted that the customer journey, documentation, and support provided to developers is important for the success of the business model. On the other hand, they also generate costs that should be seen as investment in market expansion.

It is good to stop and think about who your customer really is and what their needs and abilities are. Is it appropriate to put substantial effort into the API documentation if most customers are small online retailers with no technical expertise or resources? Such a target group is usually best served with easy access via a few clicks and add-ons for their favorite online e-commerce platforms. On the other hand, for some programmers it is challenging to directly implement unknown APIs, even if the quality of the API documentation is high.

Braintree has clearly chosen the Twilio model for voice and messaging solutions (which has also been criticized for hiding API documentation behind the code examples) and has decided to focus on minimizing the time spent by developers trying to understand the documentation. With ready-made software development kits and development environments (SDKs), one can instantly implement an application. However, the continuous maintenance of SDK and the support of new programming languages are highly labor-intensive and costly. Consider, research, and interview the target audience carefully before making large investments. One may outsource plugin development to partners but be sure to still earn some revenue; or start an open source project, whereby customers and partners work on your behalf.

The Best Business Model for Me?

The most important task in determining one's business model is to answer at least the following questions: Who is your customer, what is your value proposition, and how can you produce value for the customer at the right cost?

Numerous business models exist. In one study, Switzerland's University of St. Gallen identified 55 business models used by various companies over the past 150 years.[76] In 2013, Mark Boyd and John Musser conducted a study of the business models of APIs published at ProgrammableWeb and found about 20 business models, most of them pricing models related to revenue.[77] Hatvala (2016) researched a few Finnish companies and public organizations and found support for three business model features in companies developing APIs: open innovation, better business scalability, and IT architecture renewal.[78]

One of the most recent studies using scientific methods comes from research conducted by Wolf and Bloom (2017), where most of the interfaces studied were either priced on a transaction basis or as ancillary services to existing products or services.[79]

The Finnish government's platform economy report, which was handed over to the Government in 2016, shows that established Finnish companies have not drafted plans to take on the role of leading platform operator in their fields. Hardly any business and earnings models were making more use of digital platforms or open interfaces.

Is this really a problem then? Benzell et al. (2017) investigated the impact of APIs on the performance of companies and found that the impact of external APIs is particularly visible in market shares and valuation of companies but not so much in net turnover.[80] It is good to remember that the number of API calls or API users does not necessarily correlate directly with paying customers. In the study, they came to a somewhat surprising conclusion that internal API usage correlates best with financial results; for example, by reducing costs. However, they did not specifically investigate what interactions they made and if the APIs interacted with the network or platform business model.

So, what is the advice for one's own operations? How does the API influence business models and business model innovation? The answer is affected by whether one is developing primarily:

- A new product, technology, or service
- A single new API from a technical point of view
- An entire business strategy

If the strategy is clear, the role of the APIs in the business model is also clearer. What if the strategy has not been considered from an API point of view and your company has not decided to become a platform and open up interfaces to partners? This could result in a considerable number of headaches as a separate "IT" project.

Who Is Your Customer, What Is Your Offer, and How Do You Produce it?

The teaching of business models currently focuses on developing and describing the model using a canvas (Business Model Canvas or Lean Canvas), almost without exception. The great thing about these canvases is that they force people to think of customers as part of the business model. When done correctly, filling up the canvas even starts with customers and their needs, at least if you use the Strategyzer Value Assurance Canvas (Value Proposition Canvas) or the API value proposition canvas, which was covered in more detail in chapter 2.

Depending on the needs of the customer group from which the business model is designed, the outcome will generally be completely different from the point of view of supply and production. This is especially true for the API's role in the business model. Is the API available to end-users, or is it just a way to deliver the end-user service, the service, or the physical product? Is the API a way to enable the ecosystem to bring its own services to the platform or to provide the ecosystem with the services of its own company?

Customer-dominant Logic (CDL) is currently the the focus of service development rather than the former product- and service-oriented logic.[81] Customer-focused logic is viewed from the customer's perspective, not from that of the company's own products, services, systems, costs, or growth. The focus of customer-oriented service logic is to understand how customers can incorporate their own business offerings into their business processes. A customer-centric approach is essential to the success of the API economy, not designing solutions based on the API provider, as well as focusing on the relationship between the provider and the market.

Companies and their business models can be divided into four main categories based on resource use and scaling costs:

- Commodity builders

- Service providers
- Creators of technologies
- Network orchestrators

The biggest scaling cost of business models is for commodity builders, i.e., those who have to invest in factories, raw materials, labor, and logistics. Goods cannot be duplicated without incurring costs. Traditional service providers have a similar problem, meaning more customers always means more staff. Technology solutions are usually easier to duplicate and distribute because they are based on program code, components, and patents, but their development costs have traditionally been high and require in-depth knowledge. The network orchestrators, which also include the platform economy operators, easily beat the game both in terms of turnover and profitability, because in their business model several parties make and sell to each other.

API as a technical solution combines the business logic of both customer-focused logic (CDL) and network orchestrators. The customer can take the API as part of its own business process and build the interfaces provided by the ecosystem ("network") into the service that it wants.

The API providers can also buy APIs from others and build virtually unlimited customer journeys and new solutions. Network business models are superior to others in both revenue and scalability.

Consider a very simple example: You have a company that sells children's car seats in a local mall. Expansion would require either a huge increase in local births or the creation of new stores in different locations, which would require ample investment. Your competitiveness is based on the fact that your salesperson is well aware of the needs of families and can make good recommendations for appropriate security. Some of the customer knowledge is also related to the local knowledge of the sellers and the information about families and their preferences.

Therefore, the expansion would also require skilled sellers who are familiar with the situation in other communities. As an entrepreneur, you consider setting up an online store and transferring referral functions to it. Two options for the technical discussion are possible: to program the logic directly into the e-commerce product as customized or to make an API that offers recommendation logic using machine tools and various data sources.

What if you turn the business model into one of API economy? In that case, you could also immediately sell the recommendation API to other companies; all you need to do is enter API data from different car and seat models and classify them to suit the child's dimensions and the family needs. It's a good idea, but you need to set the API at a high price to compensate for the time it takes to retrieve and maintain data. What about all agreements with different parties on the use of information – and if the information is not correct?

If you change the business model to platform economy, profitability may be easier to achieve. For a moment, you will be wondering about the ecosystem of the safety business and the entire customer journey of the family choosing the child seat. You will find that the future need for a car seat is already known before the child is born or when the family is acquiring a new car. Thus, the customer journey and the ecosystem are those related to pregnancy and family formation, buying a car, manufacturing of car seats, market and sales, and generally to road safety. In other words, it includes everyone from family magazines for insurance companies to car seat manufacturers and the industry – globally.

Currently, there are many different sites, lists, catalogs and brochures that recommend safety seats for operators in the car seat ecosystem. Magazines make comparisons of the products and insurance companies, and the public sector knows a lot about families and even their vehicles.

In this model, you provide APIs and their terms of use for different parties to enter your information. You can forget about management contract negotiations taking place in the sauna, at the golf course, or in ski cabins and instead focus on taking care of the technical functionality and marketing of the API and the algorithm beneath it.

Summary

The essential aspects of the business model are the target groups and what kind of relationships and channels are maintained.

In the API economy, developer experience is a key part of customer experience and business model success.

The most important task of the business model is to answer at least the following questions: Who is your customer, what is your value proposition, and how can you produce value for the customer at the right cost?

Think about your business model: Is the API a way to enable the ecosystem to bring its own services to the platform or to provide the ecosystem with the services of its own company?

A customer-centric approach is essential to the success of the API economy, not designing solutions based on the API provider, as well as focusing on the relationship between the provider and the market.

Network and platform business models are best scaled both in terms of turnover and volume and results.

The API as a technical solution combines the business logic of both customer-focused logic and network orchestrators.

The customer can take the API as part of its own business process and build the service packages it wants for the interfaces provided by the ecosystem ("network").

API providers can also buy them from others and build customer paths and new virtually unlimited solutions.

SECTION II: APIS – THE LIMITED EDITION

7 CONSUME INTERNALLY – INTERNAL AND PRIVATE APIS

Marjukka Niinioja

This chapter focuses on situations in which the users of API are the organization's own personnel or developers who, on behalf of the organization, develop their own services and systems. The chapter also discusses the role of partner APIs offered by its systems to its customers and partners in ready-made systems and cloud platforms as internal interfaces when they are a key part of the implementation of an organization's services. We also look into data models and security concerns for internal APIs.

Internal APIs are often also suitable for external use. What does "internal" mean? This kind of API is often used to develop the services of one's own company; an internal API may also be available in the finished product. Product APIs are intended for use by customers and partners of the product, but this software product is mainly used to support internal processes within the organization, such as financial management, human resources management, or enterprise resource planning. The interfaces of these systems would not be provided directly by the organization to external parties, such as customers or partners, but might be used to retrieve customer information for, for example, an extranet offered to their customers.

Worldwide, API experts are feeling the heat when discussing how many API categories exist. For example, Kin Lane makes a distinction between internal and private APIs[82], while the author of the RestCase blog uses internal, partner, and public.[83]

At least a large part of the internal interfaces should be designed as if they were external. They are used on the public internet in, for example, mobile applications; these Kin Lane sets in the private API category. In RestCase's blog, the mobile application APIs are bundled with the internal network interfaces of the organization into one category: internal. In large companies, it is a reality to run into a large number of interfaces that cannot or should not be released outside the internal network. This is usually due to data protection or other legal issues. These include several APIs of public administration organizations dealing with classified information. In internal APIs, the information content is often somewhat different from that of open APIs. For example, a product API may be an API that provides basic product information; e.g., Global Trade Item Numbers (GTIN) or European Article Numbering (EAN) codes, product names, and features. If the API is used for internal purposes, it may include, for example, percentages of inventory, stock codes, or information about product coverage. It is not necessary or advisable for such information to be communicated to customers and partners and especially not to competitors.

When does the internal API stop being just internal? Who are the internal API users? They are usually very close to the developers of this API. For example, an enterprise that developed an ERP system with internal API was able to manage system settings and features more extensively than customers could. This API was practical for automating new customer deployment and automated testing. With the internal API, it was possible to change the properties of the product on the fly during testing. The API could be used for monitoring or, for example, measuring the actions taken by users. In addition, it was possible to determine at a very precise level how users used the system and how they, for example, introduced new features.

With interfaces other than the internet, there may also be limitations to who can access them or what interface is offered. For example, Apple has limited the use of NFC (Near Field Communication) for wireless communication in its phones to keep it exclusively for use by iPhone payments. In practice, APIs are interfaces provided by the phones' operating systems to enable applications to be installed on that phone to communicate with the features of a physical telephony device.

Cloud service providers provide data storage, software hosting, machine learning, and artificial intelligence services. Most of the services offered can be deployed with APIs. From the perspective of the cloud platform supplier, these APIs are directed to their customers; thus, it's a partner API. From the point of view of a customer building their own services in the cloud, these APIs are internal interfaces. With these APIs, customers implement an e-commerce or mobile application. The application implementation files are managed by the cloud platform interfaces.

You can also use your own public and partner APIs internally. In one software product, APIs were made for reporting hourly records and absences, primarily for use by customers and partners. These APIs, on the other hand, are also suitable for making new user interface implementations in modern ways: for example, with the SPA architecture (Single Page Application). It would have been impossible in the current architecture without the use of APIs.

The Distress Around Data Models

Internal APIs have their own data models. Existing requests are not optimized for any particular purpose. Thus, only basic features are provided: search all, filter, create new, change, and delete data. Often, there are also other problems in the data templates for internal APIs: structures, fields, and values are left in the API, which can be interpreted only by an expert in the subject area or are established concepts in the internal language of the company.

At worst, the solutions are inherited from a long-surviving legacy system and become a tradition that nobody dares to challenge because they "have always done it like this." No one knows how to use the API or the logic of an old system when the experts have left the company.

What's worse, every API user must ask the same things or get acquainted with complex or missing descriptions. In addition, systems using API either adopt the same incomprehensible internal data model or must do a lot of work to get their own – perhaps the more standard – data model to work with the API.

The internal APIs' data models should be questioned and considered based on common models, such as schema.org, competitors', or public-sector APIs. One should not use even those without a moment's reflection. There exist standards that should also be used for internal APIs. For example, best practice interface designs exist for names, addresses, and other contact information of companies or individuals. For internal APIs, the most common mistake is to use cryptic status and type codes: status=10 or country=16. Enumerations and other code values have not been documented anywhere. Any system using the API will have to make conversions for country codes, for example.

Country names and abbreviations should be adopted from ISO standards; dates and times are preferably handled in UTC format and time zones, as well as other standard information. It would be good to use international standards, because there is always the possibility that the company will expand abroad, or the API will be used by a non-domestic system. As a result, users will have easy access to the API, and the implementations are faster, and the errors are reduced.

Here is an example of the importance of date and time formats for internal APIs: One company was running sales operations in several countries, and their sales systems registered sales with local ERP systems. The ERP systems were located in local data centers with clocks in the time zone of that country. Sales data was collected in a centralized system (in a public cloud in a time zone different from the sales registration systems). Using API, sales transactions were searched for internal reporting and other systems by date. Because the API used the date and time information directly from the source systems and the calling system without the time zone, some of the sales remained invisible because they occurred in the "future."

Where is the Internal API Located and Who Uses it?

It would be naive to assume that the API will remain for internal use only. If the API is relatively well designed and implemented, it will suddenly attract many external users or at least software contractors working on other in-house software projects. So, don't create your API on the internal network – at least do not protect it with an internal network restriction only. Although the concept of "internal network" doesn't really exist in for many organizations, at least not for the small companies, where all services tend to already run in the cloud.

Some organizations' APIs are built to be used only within the intranet and only by trusted entities. The communication is unencrypted, and there is no user authentication at all. The internal network is not always very secure: it comes with viruses, is used by frustrated or too-curious employees, or someone accidentally opens the internal network addresses to the external firewall.

Attacks and threats aside, one of the biggest problems with unidentified API users is that no one knows who the API users really are and how to contact them. Change management and lifecycle management becomes quite challenging. If an API is disabled or if one wants to add encrypted communications or user authentication to it one day, no one can reliably say which services using API will break down and in what way. If you are using some type of API management, perhaps you know if API is used at all and if used, how much and what the API endpoints are. However, it is not known for what purpose API is used and for how long. But one will know at least whom to ask.

Running a major part of your services in the cloud is currently unavoidable. All organizations currently have to design their systems to be cloud-proof. When the cloud suddenly becomes a compulsory requirement and therefore needs to be protected by APIs, it will probably cause a lot of changes to many applications using interfaces, all of which may not even be actively maintained.

Although the API would use encrypted traffic and have some form of user authentication, not all authentication methods are cloud- or partner-resistant. The API may be protected with a simple API key or complex authentication. If you have access to the API, you will have access to all of its information and functions, as defined by your internal API.

This topic is discussed in more detail in chapter 20, but it should be noted that even a mobile application built for your own organization is like publishing your API to the general public. The source code of the mobile application is relatively easy to extract, and it's similarly easy to determine what API calls (meaning specific operations that your client applications can invoke at runtime to perform tasks) exist and its identification information. Each internal API is a potential public API. It is always worth thinking about what happens if someone outside gets their hands on the API. Suppose that the API user has all the rights to the information and functions in the system or the APIs work with the system that provides them and the access rights of the logged-in user. That, of course, should happen. It is imperative for API to provide users with access to the information and only to the functions that they would access via the system interface.

The problem arises if an API is built on APIs for customers, for example. Access rights are inherited from internal system users and are likely to be too extensive. In any case, a second data or access management layer must be applied. Licensing can also create a problem.

Direct use of the background system via API is likely to cost as much as accessing the system through the user interface, or the terms of use may allow each individual API consumer to cost as much as a normal user.

On the other hand, accessing the API with only one account can also be a matter of security or unauthorized usage. For example, the EU Data Protection Regulation requires one to know how to use personal data. Because of other laws and internal company rules, it may also be important to understand its implications for non-personal information.

Although one's goal would be to publish the API mainly to partners or the public, it is still useful to use the services used by one's own staff. Only when you are using your API will you understand what is wrong with it and how it can be developed, especially for documentation.

The first modern API (which could only be called a "RESTish API") I was involved in showed the importance of using our own API. We fortified our office with our IT team and a partner's team for a week and made plugins for a new wiki product in the new API. We came up with dozens of usability and design issues as well as bugs to fix. Lots of donuts were eaten and the office's cuddly stuffed animals got tossed about, but the API got developed and the plugin came to life. Retrospectively, the only problem in the project was the lack of market research, and perhaps the commercialization could have been a little deeper. However, the product worked well, and the API went to production even though some hiccups were discovered (which were corrected in the next completely revised version).

An even more efficient way to determine your API's development needs and especially the documentation bottlenecks is to let members from other teams put the API to use. User interface developers, report developers, consultants, vendors, and customer service representatives are potential internal API users. They can either implement new features for products or services or use it to enhance their own work. According to my experience, all the different user groups can provide good and quite different feedback.

The internal API can also be tested by enabling its use in hackathons. Even if the API is primarily internal, it can offer a lot of good ideas for more efficient operations or solutions, which in turn encourages the API provider to expand the use to other API consumers. Hackathons are also a good way to test APIs with external users. In a hackathon that lasts over the weekend, your API gets called night and day. Inadvertently, a developer finds that at 2 o'clock, the API slows down significantly (a true case from the Junction hackathon). Or someone can get your device or network blocked by your API (yet another true case from another hackathon).

Organizing internal hackathons is also a good way to model and test internal APIs. At the same time, one can think about how API and other ideas could improve work efficiency, comfort, or even responsibility or environmental friendliness. Internal hackathons are effective places for meeting people, learning new methods of working and thinking, and discovering new learning tools and motivational methods. They also work best as modern "idea box" substitutes and energize the entire work community. Internal hackathons apply to even large companies, including Google.

Does the Internal API Have a Future?

Most companies develop and use more internal APIs than external ones. On the other hand, the spread of SaaS (software as a service) and other cloud services to large companies and the public sector is causing the "internal" systems to change and move outside of the internal network. Internal API development is cost effective, while public API and partner APIs increase revenue and customer loyalty.[84]

In the future, the boundary between internal and external use may become increasingly obscure as decentralized information management (for example, block chains), cloud computing, and networked business models expand with digitalization. After all, internal and external are pretty relative concepts; it is actually about who can access what information, function, or resource through an API. The most important thing is not who uses the API or who knows about its existence. However, there are areas – such as the security, social, and health care sectors, as well as state security – where the challenge will be to meet specific safety requirements. In these areas, artificial intelligence services that are readily available from the cloud, such as image, text, or speech recognition, are not relevant. There is a need for solutions in the management of organizations where only limited individuals have access to the API or its implementation layer.

It may also happen, as it did with Netflix, that a popular public API will be converted into an internal or very restricted partner API for some time. First, the API provider gained experience with the business opportunities brought on by API, then determined which partners to use when starting the business so that close cooperation in API development is supported. Netflix had been concentrating on improving their user experience from 2012 onwards. It required the API to be used in over 300 different client applications. A separate API-layer was developed so that the user interface (UI) developers could make their own interface designs as needed. After several improvements, Netflix closed its public developer program and API in 2014.

Well-productized internal interfaces can speed up the development of services for staff, customers, and partners. Internal user groups and developers can be given the opportunity and the tools to adroitly develop and publish their own APIs but with all APIs still managed and controlled.

It would be a good idea to find an API for internal applications. However, it does not necessarily reduce the work of the integration experts and the integration platform unless the integration platform directly supports that API and, with just a few key presses, integrates it into another platform known to the API. Use of the API in other cases to build an integration always requires some programming by one of the parties. But, of course, this has often been demanded with old-fashioned file transfer at the sending and receiving end, even though it would have been passed through the integration platform with a few clicks and data transformations. Instead, the API can perform more complex functions and can be directly linked to a user interface code (at least in the case of the REST API and when the data format is JSON).

In some cases, with APIs that have already been published, it may be reasonable to limit usage to internal or well-selected partners. *"Hell hath no fury like a woman scorned,"* wrote William Cosgrove in 1695. I would like to argue that the developer community has faced the same level of social media rage when major changes have been made to a widely used API or if the API has been removed entirely.

Summary

Internal APIs are often suitable for external use and vice versa.

An internal API is often used to develop a company's own services.

An internal API may also be available in the finished product used for internal purposes.

With internal interfaces, the content of information is often somewhat different from that of external interfaces.

It is worthwhile to invest in the design of internal API interfaces and the definition of data models so that the use of API is not slowed down by legacy information and difficult terms and structures.

Once developed, internal APIs don't often remain solely in internal use or stay inside the internal network; they need security and internet capability as much as public or partner APIs.

The moment when your first mobile application is deployed to users, your API will make your internal API unintentionally public.

Use your public interfaces to develop internal services.

Organize hackathons that provide external developers with internal APIs or provide internal APIs to other teams in your company.

8 FOR THE SAKE OF PARTNERHOOD – PARTNER APIS

Jarkko Moilanen

This chapter discusses how affiliate APIs are a step forward for your business in the API economy. Partner API is a strategic decision for the company. Here, different ways of using partner interfaces in business operations are opened up through examples. In addition, the chapter provides best practices for partner API design, implementation, deployment, and iterative development.

Step into the API Economy Through Partnerships

When a company joins the API economy, it is often done by making or exploiting a partner API. However, some start their API journeys with private or internal APIs[85] and at the same time enhance their own operations and add agility and scalability. Why is that so? Hidden from the curious eyes of others, it is safe to practice. A safe start is important for an uncertain team and organization. No one wants the first exercises to be publicly discussed in various forums. (At worst, it ends up as a new meme.) Practicing also includes increasing your organization's understanding and expertise in API business models and technology. However, private and internal APIs are not really considered part of the API economy. The use of open APIs, including public and partner APIs, will take the company into the API economy.

There are two alternative strategies for utilizing partner APIs: either utilizing partner interfaces provided by others or by providing APIs for one's partners. Occasionally, a company will end up employing a combination of these over time. As such, the unilateral consumption of another company's partner APIs is quite straight forward and at its best is like being handed the API on a silver platter: Someone else has figured out how to easily implement the API, what problems it solves, and under what conditions it can be used. One should start with the easiest route and pick the low-hanging fruit, usually a product catalog, order tracking, or the like. Providing an own partner API is a more radical, and at least initially a more demanding, exercise.

However, it is good to keep in mind that it is almost impossible to predict what resources a company will open to others – i.e., to public APIs. Therefore, for internal APIs, a good rule of thumb is to approach internal APIs with the assumption that they will later be opened to others. The same idea was part of Jeff Bezos's legendary API mandate.[86] In practice, this means that the API's production process should be considered the same, including documentation that does not require insider knowledge.

Choosing a Partner

When a company decides to open an API to a partner, it is almost always a strategic decision and not one made lightly. A partner API opens up access to key processes and data to another company. Such access must be granted with care and through an agreement. For this reason, partners are usually familiar with one another.

Previously, there may have been a cooperation agreement between companies on joint marketing and recommendation. By including an API in the partnership, the level of cooperation is transferred into the everyday life of the products and services itself. Automated data processing with an API as part of business operations creates interdependence and thereby strengthens the link between otherwise loosely connected companies. The reasons behind providing a partner API are always business in nature, ones broader than just making the business more efficient. What, then, can these reasons be?

APIs Make it Easier to Expand Your Partner Network

Partner network scalability improves with APIs. With individual integrations, the expansion becomes expensive and slow. For example, the API does not lock the partner into one programming language, but the partner can use the language of their choice in their own system. The collaboration with API is not a tight integration but leaves the user enough room for maneuvering, as relates to where the data is used and how it is presented and processed. Of course, the agreement may limit the rights of the partner and determine the obligations regarding the use of the data.

Others Do the Sales

The line between partner API and other open APIs is not as strict as one might think. The two are not necessarily separate interfaces, but the functionality of API is changed based on access rights. This is the case, for example, in the Visma API solution.[87] The properties of the partner API are introduced by providing a separate parameter as part of the request. Of course, the API user account is associated with the partner permissions in Visma's access management.

The above-mentioned method is usually unsuccessful when different data models, authentication, or service-level agreement (SLA) are required. Then, a separate API is provided only for the use of partners. In the case of Visma, this type of separate solution has been provided for partners in the reseller role. In other words, what is called a partner API depends on who uses the API or on the target segment. Visma and their e-business, and ERP business, can be considered a typical digital economy business, while other more traditional industries have also moved to the API economy.

Service Business Instead of Project Business

Famous elevator company KONE, for example, is becoming more proficient in the commodity and technology industries, more and more in IT, and especially in artificial intelligence APIs. Learning from and communicating with each other, as well as maintenance services, require strong use of cognitive services through APIs and thus the building of their own APIs.[88] The service business is also transformed by the power of APIs.

Starting from partner APIs makes the KONE API strategy exceptional as compared to most Finnish companies, saying, "[...] KONE plans to encourage a vast developer ecosystem by opening Application Programming Interfaces (API's), which means new applications can be built and different types of equipment and services can be connected – creating a smoother, safer, and more personalized people flow experience for building users."[89]

By utilizing the programming interfaces, different types of information can be collected from the devices and anticipate, for example, the need for maintenance. That information can be utilized in the design of new devices to make them more durable, safer, and more efficient. Other maintenance costs can also be better optimized.

KONE itself does not produce all parts of the elevators, but they have subcontractors. APIs can automate parts ordering, delivery, and related logistics. All of this may sound small, but given the number of elevators in use, small currents grow big and small savings on time or money multiply.

Partner APIs Open Doors to New Markets

The selected partner has its own ready-made customer base. For example, by opening up one's product range, order tracking, and warehouse to a partner with API, one can expand and complement previous offerings with other products and solutions. The partnership between Kesko and Alibaba presented in Chapter 1 is a good example of this: Ali-Baba's online store provides export for Finnish products, and the market is enormous – about 488 million active users.[90] Not every customer wants pure and healthy Finnish food, but if, for example, 1% of users do buy it, that segment is almost the same as the entire Finnish population. Further, clean and traceable food is not a bad product concept. Atria, for example, has the means to trace every piece of meat back to the meadow where the cow was raised. In addition, it is possible to find out what feed the cow ate and how much. Traceability is a value for end-consumers.

Someone Has Already Solved Your Problem

A partner API can better respond to regulatory demands in a controlled manner. Monetary traffic is highly regulated, and practices vary from country to country. In this case, the partners take the regulation into account when building the service and using the information and do not have to worry about the laws of the different countries in their own API. Some examples of this are provided by Checkout Finland and Stripe, the latter of which is well known internationally and is popular with developers (as discussed in more detail in chapter 6).

More Device Sales and Better Customer Experience

The rule that a partner API must be monetized is not set in stone. A lot depends on what is the most important thing in a company's strategy. For Polar Electron, it is the promotion of device sales. Their well-known heart rate monitors, activity meters, and cycling products are for sports enthusiasts and athletes of all levels; the devices are known to almost every fitness trainer. They can monitor your heart rate and speed, collect data on performance, and a person can then use the Polar training program and utilize the analyzed data to support their exercise regimen. In addition, customers get to be a member of the community. In other words, a device is not merely "it" alone but includes the entire service experience.

Consumers want to see and use the collected performance in various ways, and the Polar online service is quite adequate for most needs. However, some consumers do not want to use the online service provided by Polar to monitor performance. As Polar strives for the best possible customer experience, however, it has thus built a partner API for key application providers, through which the device data can be exported to a wide range of popular applications such as Strava, Runkeeper, and Endomondo. In this sense, Polar's situation is reminiscent of a traditional service-oriented architecture (SOA) solution, because not all partners have the same standard API for Polar. These applications have a large user community but no devices, and for this reason, the partnership is worth its weight in gold to Polar for providing a channel to access end-users.

The strategy is understandable, because Polar focuses on the sale of the devices, but the consumer's history, habits, and needs are different. The API enables a customer who owns a Polar device to have a better customer experience by utilizing data wherever the customer prefers. Polar has made available to the various partners the necessary APIs for data transfer between systems. In discussions with Polar Electron Product Manager Jussi Mäkitervo, the other side of the free partner API emerged: "On the other hand, offering wide partner API to others is always a cost that needs to be taken into account." For this reason, the partner API is often monetized, or the fee is based, for example, on sales commission. For Polar Electron, the use of partner API does not pose a cost but is seen as a channel for new consumers, leading to increased sales of devices. At this stage of the Polar case, monetization was a pointless obstacle to the partners.

Polar doesn't think they need to do everything themselves for all target segments. Polar is looking for ways to do services with others. The example of cryptocurrencies was revealed in the conversation with Mäkitervo. Here, the user gets points for exercise in the service and can use the currencies obtained for something else via, for example, a voucher. In other words, exercise has become a currency. It is essential to understand that the Polar Electron product or API is not at the center; the most important thing is the customer and exercise experience. Mäkitervo summarized the importance of partner API in one sentence: "Polar is the best device supplier, providing, with the help of the API, the best possible sports and sports experience, produced with partners."

Polar Electro's target segment is people who actively and purposefully exercise, but the use of devices has expanded to other usage. According to Mäkitervo, insurance companies are investigating the possibility of analyzing data so profiles can be formed for different user groups (such as drivers of a particular car brand), as well as with regard to personal activity. Based on the data analyzed, business decisions can then be made, for example, regarding the content, terms, and prices of insurance. A single user may not be the target but rather it may be the larger masses in order to find attributes that are valid for most users.

What to do when the API is ready?

Once the partner API has been completed, one has just reached the beginning. One should not sit with their feet up, sighing in relief. This is just the start of the collaboration with partners in creating a new business and in producing new value with the API. Once the API is done, it may be tempting to be satisfied with the achievement and assume that the partners appear at the door as if by magic. That is not going to happen. One will probably come across a situation described by the saying, "If we build it, they won't come."[91] The partner API must also be marketed and sold.

In addition to communication and marketing, a partner program needs to be built around the API. The affiliate program includes prepared boundary conditions for the partnership, agreements, rights and obligations for each side, a revenue-sharing model, and many other things. The partner program may sound like a big deal but creating a solid framework will result in a clear process and a complete package. This reduces the burden on the organization if and when the partner API attracts a larger number of participants.

As with other types of API, a partner API must be well documented, efficient, reliable, and easy to deploy. Alternatively, in addition to documentation, it is appropriate to provide technical support, i.e., a member of an API team, to support the selected partner. This team member's job is to ensure that the partner API developer finds the documentation and understands where to start. In addition, the person you nominate will help solve unclear points and other problems if necessary. Sometimes, online collaboration is enough here, but other times, physical cooperation helps one get to the finish line faster. At this point, a skeptical reader may wonder which one is more expensive: assign one person for three days to work with the partner to kickstart new business or let one's partner survive alone for a month.

For a partner API, support services require closer connections than for an API offered to the general public. This may sound overwhelming, but it is usually a significant part of the company's strategy. You don't want the huge effort to be wasted by cutting costs in the wrong area. Keep in mind that partner API is also a service you sell and which you want the customer to benefit from easily and quickly – while your own company may have opened a new potential market through a partner.

Smart companies use an API management solution to manage API products. API management solutions often include an API analytics dashboard. Analytics can monitor the use and behavior of the API. Typically, the deviations are of interest because they induce a change that may be a sign of a nascent problem or a sign of striking gold. By tracking how partners use the API, it is possible to see trends and to come up with new business opportunities. In many cases, the simple monitoring of API analytics is not enough; business value is highlighted only by combining data sources: for example, the number of sales and level of customer satisfaction.

By following the use of a partner API, one can also see how each partner uses the API. Sometimes, the use is not optimal and may be caused by a missing feature or the fact that the partner doesn't know how to use the API effectively. In this case, the partner can be instructed to act differently or ask for more information in order to improve the API and thus reduce the number of requests and improve the partner's API experience. In the best-case scenario, through analytics one can anticipate problems, ones that would usually lead to a decrease in revenue and benefits.

Is there life after partner API development?

What about when a partner API is created and running? In many cases, the company does not change very quickly – in a more open direction – but rather (and rightly) utilizes the partner API more widely and efficiently, acting as both the provider and the consumer.

Occasionally, the need arises for a more open model than the partner API. Sometimes, the lessons learned, and the benefits gained will serve as a springboard for launching open APIs, which do not always mean the open data APIs. The company gains the courage to make a leap towards openness. Courage has been gained, because revenue has been generated through partner API, trust in one's own know-how has grown, and mistakes have been reduced through experience.

Summary

The key messages in this chapter are:

APIs make it easier to expand your partner network.

It is worth providing a partner API, assuming that it will at some stage be opened up for the use of a wider audience.

Partner API is a strategic corporate decision that significantly affects the company's sales.

Each industry can benefit from the use of well-designed and targeted partner API.

Finding new business opportunities is possible by analyzing the partner's API usage.

9 APPLY EXTERNALLY – PUBLIC API

Mika Honkanen

This chapter discusses public programming interfaces. The chapter also looks at interfaces for open data distribution. In addition, the benefits and disadvantages of the business are discussed. The chapter contains many practical examples from Finland and around the world.

Benefits offered by public API interoperability have been the guiding principle of internet development throughout its existence. The principles of interoperability were developed in the modular design of computers in the 1950s. The first public APIs were the eBay Developer Toolset in 2000, the Amazon Web API, and the Google Search API in 2002. Initially, these first public APIs allowed a very limited number of requests and queries, as well as a very limited amount of information. Subsequently, the restrictions were reduced, and more information was made available through API.

According to the Metcalfe Act of 1993, as presented by George Gilder, the value of the network is proportional to the square of the number of endpoints on the network. The API that no one uses is useless, but the value of the ten API networks (102=100) is 25-fold compared to the two API networks (22=4). As the network grows, the benefits will grow rapidly as long as the API initially creates value for the network. For this reason, whenever a new API is associated with a network, the benefits of the entire network will increase. Public API provides the opportunity for third-party developers to utilize it in their own applications.

The public API, along with the partner API, belongs to the open API category and allows seamless communication of services and applications with each other. (For more information on API categories, see chapter 7.) The public API makes digital content more widely available in various services. When the existence of API is publicly visible beyond the organization and stakeholders, it also acts as a marketing tool for the wider public. With public API, an organization can expand into multiple applications and ecosystems and gain greater awareness of its products. API marketing is a critical step in expanding its use. Publicly marketed, the market can garner much more and faster constructive feedback, so publicity can be used as a strategic means to learn and develop faster.

One way to perceive the growth of public APIs is to look through the API catalog services. Founded in 2005, ProgrammableWeb lists almost 20,000 public APIs in its catalog service as of February 2018. (The catalogs and their role in the API economy were discussed in more detail in chapter 3.)

The public programming interface can be used both internally and externally. The same interface can provide a wider version internally or for partners (partner API) and a more limited version publicly. The use of public API is also recommended within the organization, as the API will usually develop and function better, and the organization will be more aware of related issues. If necessary, API can be prioritized in networking and capacity, whereby the same API can be used by different groups of users for which API can provide a different level of service and functionality.

The external use of API again means that APIs are also exploited by software developers and other external users from outside the organization. For example, Google's search engine API can be used by anyone, not just Google employees. Or, the meteorological API of the Finnish Meteorological Institute can be used by a private company outside the public administration.

With a public interface where no authentication has been used, it may be difficult to collect information about its users. For example, API analytics may report that the interface is requested from cloud services (from the internet service provider's IP address), so it may be very difficult to determine who actually uses the interface. In addition, the new EU General Data Protection Regulation hinders the collection and processing of personal data. In Finland, for example, the law has been interpreted as meaning that dynamic (variable) IP addresses are also personal information.[92] For example, some personal information is often requested for an API key, such as GitHub, Facebook, a Google profile, or a user name and email address. As a result, API users form a register containing personal information.

Although the API is public, it should always be designed to suit a specific use. Therefore, it is important to limit the goals and target groups in public API design. On the other hand, it is good to keep in mind that an API's business model can be highly innovative. There are an increasing number of business models and strategies for API[93], presented in more detail in chapter 6.

Business Opportunities for Public API

An organization can utilize public interfaces in two ways: by consuming existing interfaces of others or by developing their own interfaces. One should consider what is already available and how to use it as part of one's organization. Open data interface, which should not be confused with the open API, has been published for use by citizens and companies by the public administration in Finland. Their existence is rarely known, because the administration has little visibility.

For example, the World Bank decided to publish its data via public API in 2010.[94] Currently, it offers three open data APIs. The first offers more than 8,000 indicators, some of which are available for the previous 50 years. The second API provides information on World Bank projects (completed, ongoing, and planned). The third provides information on World Bank loans and credits.[95]

Often, the public interface can be used free of charge ("free model") up to a certain limit. When the amount of usage exceeds that limit, the interface becomes chargeable, as is the case with Google Map API.[96] Hobby and experimental use of an API's free capacity is often enough, but excessive use is charged. Use of the public interface may incur a cost, and the data provided by the interface is not necessarily transparent. There may be different contracts and pricing models for the use of API and the use of data provided by API.

Free API creates more opportunities for innovation. Many startup companies utilize open data to develop their own business models and consider it important that open data produced by public administration is available and published free of charge.[97] In Finland, for example, Ultrahack, Eduhack, Junction, Hyvinvointihack, and Industryhack competitions have all utilized open data and various interfaces.

The information produced by public administration is, in principle, open and accessible to the public. For the platform economy, this is a very good thing. For example, an entire country can make use of public trading interfaces and other open software culture and internet tools to promote the platform economy and thus its competitiveness.[98]

For example, the Meteorological Institute provides weather information via an API. Weather data can help one save energy in building heating or optimize traffic in many ways. Weather data is therefore valuable information, is also available through public interfaces, and is offered by many commercial operators. Thus, it is always necessary to carefully consider when a public operator provides a public service or related information and when it comes to a service that competes with commercial providers.

The National Board of Patents and Registration provides some of its information through an open data interface, making it possible to gather information about businesses. This should be used regularly by every company in its operations. Information is also important for the public administration, which purchases from and cooperates heavily with companies and organizations.

In Finland, all major cities have hundreds of information systems and huge amounts of data. For example, there are about 200 information systems in Vantaa and around 700–900 in Helsinki, depending on the method of calculation. It is no secret that cities do not even know what information is in their databases. The same situation applies to the state administration: a lot of information exists, but nobody knows exactly what is available in digital format.

In addition to the public sector, the overall picture is lacking in many companies. In recent years, businesses have focused on managing core data rather than trying to get all the information under control. Finland's six largest cities have created APIs in a project called "6Aika," the goal of which is to create a unified interface, regardless of which city resources are involved. Four unified interfaces have been published so far: the resource reservation interface allows one to search for urban spaces and tools; the event interface allows one to search for and see all events in cities; the decision-making interface can be used to monitor urban decision-making and to find related information; and the feedback interface facilitates input on urban infrastructure.

Open Public Administration

The Finnish public administration is governed by the Act on the Openness of Government Activities (21.5.1999/621), the first section of which (disclosure principle) states that "documents of public authorities are public unless otherwise provided by this Act or another Act." In practice, this means that the public administration operates openly by default if there is no legal reason to restrict the transparency of the information.

As a result of the open principle, the public administration has also opened up a large amount of data resources as "open data." Open data refers to that in machine readable form, often the only condition for which is that its original source be mentioned. The world's most commonly used definition is: *"Open data (content) is allowed to be freely used, edited, and shared by anyone for any purpose, provided it mentions its original source."*[99]

In accordance with open data thinking, the public administration should provide a platform for publishing data from government registers free of charge and in machine-readable form so that the greater society can utilize it for different needs. This supports the idea that the state is such a platform.[100] This is the same idea as physical infrastructure, where the state builds and maintains a road network that is then used by other parties. Criticism has been raised against the idea of the state as a platform, that it restricts the role of the state as a provider of only data ("raw material") and assumes that the private sector generates most of the value.[101] Since the data has been opened on the CKAN platform (e.g., the national www.avoindata.fi portal), it is also available for download via API. The CKAN software is fully API-designed and implemented.

Open Data API

The Open Data API refers to an API in which the data content itself is open. Generally, open content means that the content is licensed under an open data license. In Finland, Open Knowledge Finland and COSS have jointly created and maintained the definition of an open interface, which despite small differences in perspective can be seen as a definition of an open data API.[102] It is essential to understand the difference between an open API (public and partner) and open data API. At its purest, the open data API sets these three requirements:

1. It is offered for free.
2. Everyone has access to it.

3. The content provided by the API is provided free of charge under license.

A good example of a well-implemented open data distribution API since 2004 has been the Finnish Transport Agency's Digiroad, whose task is to distribute open data from the national road and street network. Digiroad offers a comprehensive, unified description of the transport network in machine-readable form.[103] It is possible to build various route planning, navigation, travel, and traffic telematics services on it. For example, an application has been implemented over the interface to conveniently view train arrival and departure information in real time.

In the private sector, Fingrid Oy opened its own open data services in February 2017. The Finnish company – which is responsible for electricity transmission in the main grid, takes care of electricity connections abroad, and promotes the operation of the electricity market – provides open data on the electricity market and power system. Their site is built on top of the CKAN open-source data portal software, whereby all open data on the service is also available through API.

Although an API is a public or even an open data API, so easily accessible and with little restriction to use, it will often be of no interest to software developers without good documentation and testing capability, a common challenge for open data APIs. For example, the Open Data API of the National Board of Patents and Registration is very illogical in its data model and restricting queries (300 minutes per user among all users). It takes at least a week to retrieve all open data. For many developers, Statistics Finland's open data API is very difficult to use. The same challenge lies in the Meteorological Institute's API. There has been a lot of discussion on the 4,000-member-strong open data Facebook groups. API data models are perceived as highly expert-oriented, so they do not easily lend themselves to use by third parties.

Many open data APIs lack a user- and application-developer-oriented perspective. In principle, data has been opened as open data, but its use is technically challenging and laborious for application developers. In other words, the developer experience has not been well thought-out and implemented. For more on developer experience, see chapter 16.

Permission to use the content provided by the API may have a different license than the interface itself. The API can be seen as a gateway to access the information, and the gateway (the interface) and the information (its contents) are different things. On the other hand, the exploitation of information is limited by copyright, related rights, and similar restrictions. The interface information always involves a license and copyright, even if it has not been specifically identified. The high-quality programming documentation (and content) clearly states how the content provided by the interface is licensed and how to use it.

An internationally significant transparency license is the Creative Commons license family. Creative Commons offers six different licenses, of which only one (CC BY 4.0) meets the criteria for open data. It is a worldwide standard for open data publishing. Generally known and used licenses are trustworthy for different parties, as they have typically been dealt with several times in court and have been subject to extensive case law. Therefore, it is often not worthwhile to set up one's own data usage terms; rather, one should define the data license according to commonly used licenses.

In Finland, public administration has often licensed its own dataset with the JHS-189 license, which is internationally compatible with the Creative Commons 4.0 license. In practice, the JHS-189 is the Finnish version of this international license.[104]

If the material is even partially covered by the protection of copyright or related rights, but the publisher wishes to waive all of its exclusive rights, he may use CC0 (CC zero). CC0 is the recommended license for the interfaces data model and structure descriptions (for example Open API standard definitions). It is advisable to license metadata with a CC0 license so that it can be automatically listed in the API catalogs by a software robot.

Open Business Opportunities with Open Data APIs

It is often thought that if information is shared openly, then it is not possible to do business with it. Partly, this thinking drives organizations to pledge their own information sacred and close their doors as far as possible. Organizational culture does not necessarily support transparency, and sometimes it is feared that important capital of an organization will be lost via an open data API. These clashes between the business model, technical solutions, and organizational culture are discussed in chapter 11. On the other hand, open data APIs also provide a useful way to find qualified employees. Many software professionals in Finland and around the world have built open data applications.

Finland-based Mårten Mickos, who sold the MySQL open source database product for billions of dollars to the United States, stated that he knew nothing better than anyone else about how to do business with open source (transparency) – the most important thing is to invent it yourself, and there are certainly a lot of opportunities.[105] Often, there is no ready-made formula or model; creativity must be utilized. This is the same for both public and open data interfaces and more generally for the API and platform economy.

Summary

Google, eBay, and Amazon created the first public online APIs in the early 2000s.

Public APIs create ecosystems and enable open innovation.

The number of public APIs is growing strongly. For example, ProgrammableWeb lists over 20,000 APIs.

The Public Interface is a partner API, which is another classification of open interfaces.

Open data interfaces, in turn, are used to distribute open access data.

Public and open data APIs offer the opportunity to expand one's business, market one's products, or communicate brand or employer image.

Businesses should explore what programming interfaces the public administration offers and how they can be used develop one's business.

An organization may have two roles when it comes to public interfaces: provider and user.

Open public data in the Finnish public administration can be found on the avoindata.fi website. All information on the site is also accessible via an API.

10 THE DEVELOPER COMMUNITY AS CUSTOMER

Jarkko Moilanen

This chapter discusses the diversity of the user community (B2D) in relation to the traditional target market, i.e., the end-users of digital services. API consumers, that is, application developers, require their own direct and sales-jargon-free practices to deal with an API offering. Usually, the dialogue with the users culminates in the Developer Portal, the goal of which is to help the consumer understand the value added by APIs and provide the means for quick deployment.

Igniting Passion and Creativity

As a target segment, API consumers are different from end-customers, who use the outputs of the API consumers. It is no wonder that big companies have community managers on staff, managing the interaction between the community and the company. If you use API Canvas[106] for a business-oriented design, you will find that some of the sections of the canvas deal with the developer relationship (This issue is discussed in more details in Chapters 2 and 12). The developer relationship describes how to find, deploy, and interact with an API, as well as what channels you use to distribute the API. In short, one can talk about a developer program.

The most prominent feature of developer programs is often the developer center, which is usually a portal that provides all the essentials for utilizing your APIs.[107] A good developer center offers a step-by-step journey to the point where the user employs the API in their own application and possibly sells the resulting product to consumers. For Nordea's Open Banking Developer Center, this is done in three steps: 1. The developer registers his or her application. 2. He or she tests and finalizes the application and API interaction with the sandbox against test data. 3. He or she asks permission to connect to production data. All other content and functions in the center provide support for this process.

The developer programs make it possible to innovate and produce new products in collaboration with those outside the company. In Chesbrough's words, innovation takes place outside of your own organization.[108] Keep in mind, however, that at the heart of thinking is not the product but what API consumers can do with your APIs. The goal is not to get others to work for you but to do it with co-creation. If you want to get developers on your side, ignite their passion and creativity, support and maintain their journey, and make it possible to do business.

In developer marketing, it is not enough for the API to be introduced (paid or free) and for the consumer of the API to feel that they get something out of it. In addition, one must consider the end-customer of the process and their satisfaction with the application or service in which your API plays a key role. Before one can develop an efficient and relevant developer program, one must get to know the target audience: in this case, the consumers of the API.

From Innovators to Laggards

Application developers, that is, typical API consumers, are easily categorized as geeks. However, API consumers, such as application developers, are not made from the same mold, because some of them are just starting their careers and some of them are advanced contenders.

Their interests range from developing innovations to utilizing ready-made productized APIs. In addition to these extremes, there are a number of developers who are not interested in web interfaces for one reason or another.

The API consumer community can be divided into five customer segments as defined by Rogers (2010):[109] innovators, early adopters, early majority, late majority, and laggards. Except for the final segment, each plays their own roles and has their own needs in developing and using APIs. Therefore, these segments should be taken in to account. Innovators are happy to ride the hype curve in search of new, innovative solutions and technologies. They can be your window to the future and help with APIs and business in long-term strategic planning.

Early adopters are a bunch of API consumers who may have experience with product owner work. They may have an insight into what mass-consumers of your API require. With their help, you can cross the so-called Moore's chasm[110] and succeed in the mass market. Moore added the chasm into Roger's model between the early adopters and the early majority. The peculiarity of the chasm is that pre- and post-chasm segments have very different expectations and needs for the implementation of products and services. To overcome the chasm, the API developer and customer experience must be put right.

For the last couple of years, I have been in close contact with those using APIs as part of the development of making API management solution as development-friendly as possible. In these discussions, it has been made crystal-clear that the early majority's expectations for the API are that it is efficient, reliable, and easy to use. The early majority and late majority include those consumers (users) who are typically seen as paying customers. According to their name, these groups contain the lion's share of users and are therefore attractive target groups for commercial APIs. The aim, therefore, is to get on the right side of these segments!

Developers' interests differ greatly; their interests vary over time, and the scale is wide. Some may be interested in producing tools for other developers and some in working with artificial intelligence, while others focus their time on social media or payment transactions. Not all developers can be a target market for one's APIs: your solutions are perhaps simply not of interest for one reason or another. Because resources in marketing or product development are usually limited, the target group must also be limited.

The rest of this chapter discusses ways to improve cooperation with the community and build a developer program for your API or API family.

Empathize with Developers

Once the segmentation of API consumers for the API has been done and the challenges in providing services through APIs have been clarified, one can move on. A good API does what it promises and does it well. In order to properly position your API in the market, you need to understand the context in which the API is used. One must determine where in the various digital services the API can add value to the developer and the end-customer of the service. Ask yourself: Who are the real consumers of this API? How can I make life easier for them? What brings them value almost immediately?

Consumers of the API rarely use it "just because"; usually, there is a reason. Developers' motivations have been studied from different perspectives in the past and understanding them is an integral part of successful APIs. Motivation can be studied on two levels: internal and external.

An example of internal motivation is *"scratch your own itch"*[111] which, among other things, has been found in open source communities as one of the key motives for participating in projects. The API consumer may have the same motive: API resolves a problem faced by the consumer as a part of a whole solution developed by the consumer. The difference with open source is that the consumer does not necessarily have to do a similar amount of work to solve the problem.

Another internal factor is the desire to learn new things. Application developers are known for self-study during the evenings and weekends. The developer may, along with a few beers on a Saturday, pick up your APIs and try different things with it. Then, when he arrives at the office on Monday morning, he tells the team that the desired function can be implemented with the API and that he has already performed a Minimum Viable Product implementation.[112]

Examples of external factors are the creation of business with API (commercial application) and the achievement of the organization's goals with the API (although internal motivation may be involved).

Like Peeling Onions

An API consumer community is created around the API, and its members can be aware of each other. The size of the community and the relative proximity of the members vary. Typically, the community structure is such that only a very small number of people are strongly committed and directed. There are some contributors, but the largest part consists of just followers. The owner of an API can influence the formation and increase awareness. At best, this leads to a community that starts to organize itself and act as ambassadors for API, attracting new consumers.

From the point of view of the owner of the API, the community created around the product is the most interesting, because they utilize the API and are the most natural party for providing feedback and to pay for the API. Feedback can come through inquiries, but a more modern way is to enable a dialogue between the provider and the consumers of the API. In addition, information about developer experience and the API should be collected through monitoring.

The API provider can contain the conversation to a specific location but does not block conversation elsewhere. For example, the owner can set up a discussion forum in his own developer center or take advantage of existing platforms such as Stack Overflow. According to one small-scale study, consumers often (50% of the time) find answers sooner on Stack Overflow than from the official documentation.[113] As such, this is not surprising, and I myself have often found the answer elsewhere than through official routes. The same has been said by API consumers I have interviewed.

The developer community, of course, exists outside the scope of influence of your API, and it also absorbs influences from other sources. Understanding only the needs of your existing API developer community leaves the company on thin ice. The above is a product-oriented perspective for the community. Another aspect is the position of the individual members in the developer community, which also applies to the product perspective community.

In addition to the actual APIs, you must also consider the managers who generally lead application teams and make decisions. Documentation cannot be written only for code-level users but also for managers and other potential decision-makers. Typically, managers are interested in the reliability of the API, what kind of risk factor it forms for the whole solution, whether the providing organization is reliable, and the future of the API. The same problem with the two segments also applies to the developer center. The challenge is that what appeals to developers is not necessarily appealing and traction-inducing in the eyes of their managers.

Developers are Lazy, and Time is Precious

I started my presentation at the DevOps 2017 event with a slide that read *"Developers are Lazy Bastards."* The purpose was to awaken about 300 DevOps professionals who'd sat down to listen after lunch. It obviously worked, because eyebrows went up and a fair amount of electricity enlivened the air.

The subject of my presentation was automation and acceleration of the API production process and cost savings. The situation resolved quickly, and the dialogue with the public began. It was not the provocative title of the slide that was essential but the hidden message it contained: the appropriate amount of laziness makes us more efficient. The same applies to API consumers. An API made by someone else is used because it generates added value, and often there is no reason to engineer a solution from scratch. Reinventing the wheel is a waste of time and effort.

The consumers of an API do not want to learn things the hard way, and they usually do not even have the time to do so. Therefore, make the API easy to understand and deploy. Solving customer problems is what brings added value. One's APIs are not the only things the consumer spends their time on; he or she may have dozens of APIs to work with. The consumers therefore have no time to get to know the soul and intricacies of each API.

That's why serious effort should be put into making the API clear and easy to use. Comprehensive documentation must be available, but the basic use of the API and the first experience of success cannot hinge upon reading 50 pages of documentation. From the point of view of the consumer in this case, the software developer sees intuitiveness, reliability, and ease of use as essential, because it minimizes time and effort. The same is true for the managers above the consumers, who often make decisions about whether to use the API or not. Managers often have tight schedules for completing a project, and the product needs to be delivered to the customer or market as quickly as possible.

One of our authors, Marjukka Niinioja, experimented with the developers' reactions when briefly exposed to four different developer centers at an API event. Impressive-looking sites sparked the question, "Do I need to talk to the salesperson next?" For developers, portals can be visually appealing, but the style of the message should be chosen correctly.

It is more of a question of wording and of the mental images that arise. Developer portals are often designed by the same group of marketing people who have spent the last 20 years thinking about how to approach the end-consumer and how to sell the product. For developers, the same things are no longer valid. Developers usually don't like very marketing-friendly materials.

One of the worst mistakes that can be made is to put a contact form next to the API, through which the API key or other information is provided – and the sales department contacts you after you submit. If the first response really needs to be from a salesperson, he or she should be familiarized with Business to Developers (B2D) marketing.

Another option is to use a community manager, if there is one in the company. The consumers of the API do not want to encounter a situation where they don't get immediate access to the API but are first targeted by the vendors' telephone and email terror. Or, in the worst-case scenario, no one gets in touch at all. Less is usually more, meaning that the simpler the material, the more the impression is conveyed that the developer does not need to see a salesperson and that the site is properly provided with technical information and documentation.

Developers want to get information clearly and without the feeling of being forced to buy something. In that sense, the somewhat raw approach tends to work better. Of course, it should be remembered that what does not appeal to the developer may appeal to the manager above him.

For developers, content marketing works. Produce content that helps them understand the API's use and potential. When considering texts, one has to consider that the main point is not the API but a solution to a problem and how to execute it easily.

The Expanding Developer Community

The discussion above is mainly about the group of people who code every day. As the APIs become more common, the consumer community also changes. One trend currently spreading is the idea that coding skills are no longer so important – i.e., low-code and no-code platforms. Their existence and success are mainly based on general-purpose open and free interfaces.

Some readers may have used the Zapier or If-This-Then-That service (IFTTT) to automate tasks or events in their daily lives, such as email, social media, digital image storage, and home automation (IoT devices).[114] These platforms utilize the interfaces of the services connected to it and allow their sharing without coding. These platforms, called no-code solutions, do not require coding skills. As a result of this development, the use of the API in integrations goes beyond the tool for developers, although the API is hidden and productized so well that the user knows nothing about it.

Low-code platforms, such as Devslab, have at least not yet gained such popularity as IFTTT and Zapier. In contrast to the no-code-platform – where, as a rule, only a mouse is clicked to set the functions – some coding skills are required on the low-code platform. In turn, the low-code platform poses a higher degree of freedom, because the platform administrator has not limited the usage scenarios.

Summary

The key messages in this chapter are:

If you want to get developers on your side, ignite their passion and creativity, support and smooth their path, and enable business.

The members of the consumer community are interested in different issues and have different starting points.

Time is valuable, including for developers, and developers are lazy in a smart way.

In addition to developers, you need to understand their managers.

Understand the everyday life of the consumer and their problems and then create solutions for them.

Understanding the developer's motives (internal and external) is an essential part of successful interfaces.

SECTION III: THE LEAN LEAP TO APIS

11 APIS CHANGE YOUR ORGANIZATION

Marjukka Niinioja

This chapter discusses the impact of APIs on an organization's internal operations, offering new paths, a reconfigured division of labor, novel strategies, and optimized interactions. In short, the API economy is changing the way one procures, sells, and offers services, thus lending change to the nature of management and the types of people and skills needed.

Ecosystems have a significant impact on software development. This is especially the case if the development approach is changed from integration- or product-centric to service-oriented. APIs and API management are often perceived as either integration or a byproduct of the development of digital services and microservices. Integration experts working alongside traditional systems and integration platforms are under pressure to understand the API world. Software developers working on the edge of the microcomputer at the edge of the cloud do not understand how to work with the internal network and ERPs.

One challenge in the API economy includes the fact that management, sales and marketing, personnel development, and other support functions must understand what one needs in order to communicate, market, and sell to customers, as well as what kind of expertise one should recruit. Process, service, and project managers and architects, on the other hand, are struggling with whether to do things in an agile or traditional way, should they get on board with the much-hyped new methods of work.

It is essential to understand that in the API world, the services and their users are the talk of the town, whether internal or external, paying or not. API is the interface that provides resources to different parties as services. *May the users do what best fits their needs*–types of integrations are about "agreements," which must be mutual and cover the following:

1. What does each party provide and in what format? (For example, a file with customer information or a more traditional web service, REST API, or other data source that can be used to query customer information.)

2. What will be done with the incoming information? (Will it be moved to the edge of a hard disk, will it be converted to another format, or will it be mapped to the interface of another system? Which field matches which, and how often should the data be transferred?)

Thus, there are always two parties in the integration, and the object is the data that is transferred to and converted for the parties.

The API, on the other hand, is like an electric socket: it transfers a specific amount of data or functions. However, the API wants to know what that data really is and to provide certain possibilities for processing said data. In addition, the data is merely a way for the API to communicate with the resources that use it, which can be very varied and multifaceted, as described in the previous chapters.

The API itself is not integration; it lacks the second party of the agreement (though the number of parties can be unlimited). However, the API does not know anything about the parties other than being registered as API consumers. APIs from different parties are unable to communicate directly with each other; for example, the software developer can call the API from the mobile application's code.

There may be a need for an integration tool (and possibly an expert) to make the APIs talk to each other.

During one API training, the integration expert summed up what he has learned as follows: *"APIs have users just like user interfaces. And just as usability studies are performed for users of user interfaces, so must it be done for API users (consumers). That is the big difference between an API and an integration!"*

Integration orientation may have some significant side-effects compared to service-centricity. Researchers Bosch and Bosch-Sijtsema (2010) emphasize in their reference framework the consideration of the interaction between architecture, processes, and organization.[115] According to their research, the development of unified software products has spread across a wide range of areas, causing cultural, linguistic, and competence challenges. These will cause problems when scaling up local enterprise software development and interaction techniques for use by teams around the world.

In the current wave, software ecosystems are being provided alongside internal development teams and their software platforms, for which external developer teams are developing their own services. As stated in previous chapters and in the Bosch & Bosch-Sijtsema study, one can hear the emphatic voices of these external developers when discussing development plans, schedules, and other matters related to the whole platform and its services.

The globalization of operations, the growth of networked working methods, the development of technology, and the acceleration of development are also key factors in the development of digitalization. The power of the API to change the nature of an organization is thus two-sided: organization's internal API development causes change from within while, on the other hand, the opportunity offered by APIs to integrate external parties to company's innovation and service processes is increasing. Such change enables and forces organizations to open up and think about means and conditions for interacting with external developers, ecosystems, and interfaces with providers of their services.

APIs Do More Than Just Change IT

APIs do not just change information management or software development and product development; they also change how an organization acquires and oversees its services and how its budgeting, management, and outsourcing of services and resources operate.

Studies have investigated what happens in an organization when it starts to develop APIs and employ interfaces. The change and its magnitude depend in part on intent. Indeed, Lewis and Lewis have been examining the changes to open innovation – caused by public APIs and partner APIs – currently underway in the media sector.[116] For example, an external developer had built a free iPhone application using National Public Radio's (NPR) API, which quickly became popular. The developers of NPR heard about the application and hastened to make their own. This is just one possibility, however. NPR also could have built a revenue-sharing model for the content and allowed third parties to manage and own the applications, if such monetization had been possible (based on its financial and ownership structures).

Therefore, an organization no longer needs to invent and experiment with all the ideas itself but can learn from outside developers. Aitamurto and Lewis also emphasize APIs' impact on accelerating internal product development, such as that of UK newspaper the *Guardian*. According to their research, APIs provide more structured tools for product development and more time for teams to focus on user experience. The study also revealed that APIs accelerate collaboration across organizational units.

In the organizations investigated by Aitamurto and Lewis, commercialization was done using APIs, especially in the *Guardian*'s case.

There, the vision of the entire organization was built heavily on the idea that it is not enough for a company to be *on* the internet; it must be *part* of the internet. The company shared its content with an API, and developers were able to use it on their own sites. The shared content included the *Guardian* ads, and developers could also use it to share their own ads. The overall strategy was to transform the website into a news platform.

The above benefits and results from accelerating and commercializing product development do not arise without the participation of API consumers and community. In the study by Aitamurto and Lewis, it was found that APIs, especially when provided as self-service, more easily and quickly help establish a larger network and community. Indeed, the community has created partnerships and business opportunities for news organizations. Some organizations have begun to actively feed their community by organizing various events (e.g., hackathons) where developers and news providers meet and collaborate. Based on these encounters, an organization is also able to gain a better understanding of its own needs for expertise in producing new innovations.

However, the change from closed innovation to open is not straightforward. Conservative organizational culture in particular slows API utilization. There persists an assumption that one can do without any APIs when they have not been needed previously. In the study by Aitamurto and Lewis, other challenges raised were copyright of information and the mindset that content published through public API is always free, transferring the value creation outside the organization.

The developers highlighted favorable solutions in their research to convince management: they sold the "limited openness" perspective and the "Business 2.0" concept. Thus, it would be better to control what someone can already automatically "scrape" from the content of the web pages. Further, such a situation presents the opportunity to get to know who the users are, to identify the possibility to receive advertising revenue, and to form partnerships.

Introducing Your Organizational Change

An API expert is called to the scene when technical solutions and instructions are needed or at least assumed to be needed. Most API-planning organizations also require another element, as was seen from the previous Aitamurto and Lewis research: they need a partnership strategy that governs the transparency of networks and platforms rather than (or supplementary to) the API strategy. An alternative is to develop a business strategy that considers the digitalization and competitive situation that identifies one's own or the partners' APIs as one of the services and competition or production factors offered.

APIs can change an organization's strategy, but then many other changes will often be needed in the organization's culture, interaction, skills, and responsibilities. This sounds like years of change – a demanding management-involved and system-wide challenge, right? The truth, however, is that on the day the organization starts to set up the first APIs, organizational change is inevitable.

Let's first look at how an API-free organization works. It may not be a worse example but clearly different. For example, with a startup consisting of one team with a few coders who develop their first product, the pace is fast, and the team is given ideas daily about new features customers have requested, ones competitors have invented, or what the organization itself has needed for similar products. Not much architecture exists or needs to be thought of when surfing the next wave of hype if something that works is delivered. Generally, then, outputs are obtained where all the code is the same: the user interface, action logic, and database code are entangled. Nothing can be done before the user interface is designed or the database exists.

It takes a long time to implement the changes, because they are done sequentially. The duration, risks, and impact of the changes are only seen at the end, when the previous layers are first implemented, and half of the project time and resources have already been used. This causes organizational "silos" to form, because experts from different disciplines (such as business application specialists, data scientists, API developers, and network specialists) don't understand each other, even though they are all working within "IT." The motivation to cooperate can't be forced; it needs to be innate.

So, first, one should plan the interfaces, which some also call the data model. Everyone can comment on them, including the user interface designers; the testing, application, database or analytics experts; and external developers. Once everyone has studied the interface description, they can start using the interface in their own work.

Communication is done through interface definitions, which is like an agreement or promise between different parties. When virtually nothing of the interface yet exists, other than the definition, changes are implemented quickly and without challenges. It is easy to let the first API consumers know when the specification changes, as it will immediately appear in the interface implementation. An interface can be prototyped, provided as "executable" without the underlying services being implemented. This will greatly improve the speed and responsiveness of the organization and is very important for its productivity, performance, and culture. Interfaces and the way they share and synchronize work help clarify and develop an organization's needs and ability to communicate with other teams and individuals. This removes silos, a crucial step.

Suddenly, there is a tool for everybody – including business and otherwise "non-technical" people – a tool understood by most and largely in the same way. Based on the API definition, other teams can implement a user interface, automated test cases, application logic, or the database.

So, what does this change really mean? Well, let's consider a story.

Once upon a time, a huge company existed. It had at least hundred project teams developing different systems and solutions at the same time. There was hardly any communication or exchange of information between the project, because there was no compulsion to do so. Perhaps an architect or expert had at one point noticed that different projects dealt with the same challenges but produced completely different solutions. Or, when the production stage was reached, one noticed that some other functionality got broken, but it was outside the boundaries of the project.

All the project teams and business units were able to live in their own architectural bubbles and the different suppliers of the projects able to implement completely separate solutions. These "islands" then surfaced suddenly while discussing architecture for a new project, and the architects rolled their eyes and sighed deeply.

What, then, happens to all those siloed teams when an organization builds APIs? Suddenly, all teams can talk to each other. In fact, they have no choice.

A human is basically a social animal. Often a "must" can be converted to a "need," and the ability to discuss alternatives and experiences with other teams becomes a pleasure. Often, experts and architects have had to work alone, i.e. "independently," but they are often happier solving things together and giving and receiving feedback. In professional work, it is generally important for people to be able to create sensible solutions and in the end feel proud of their work.

Each team carries out its own little piece of a larger puzzle and creates its own API implementations for a limited need. Alternatively, the team uses APIs provided by other teams and possibly external providers to do their own work; for example, an application or service. Some may call these feature teams[117], others product, solution, or even customer teams. What matters is that each team is suitably independent and responsible for its own product or service or, as we learned in previous chapters, from its resources. These resources can provide a variety of sensible solutions. The internal and external teams that combine the APIs into solutions are customers of these "resource teams." On the other hand, an organization can also utilize external APIs or external resource teams to produce them.

Let's return for a moment to the idea of the whole organization communicating and the different teams being dependent upon one another. Such dependencies may even sound like a risk, but the real risk (or the biggest opportunity) involved is that everyone suddenly understands what is being done and how they relate to each other across the organization, services, and projects.

The change does not happen by itself, and it does not happen overnight. At first, it requires full-time facilitation, but at some point, one will find that things and people "simply work" in a new way, without daily reminders.

A Real-world Example of a Sweeping Business Change

I worked as Development Manager at Kesko from 2016 to 2017, where API creation was only then being integrated as part of the development of certain services. Two teams existed, and APIs were just one part of their focus. The first initial API team worked for several months before being able to publish the first APIs. The biggest challenges were to not only get the organization to understand what APIs are and what they are not but also to determine what interfaces would be needed first. The internal customers of these early APIs were several project teams, and the architectural designs were quite general. At the very least, a product API, a store API, and a customer API would be needed. But what features should they offer? In what order should they be done? Which project would fund the development?

Discussions with different parties and project teams were required in order to gain an understanding of what features each party was expecting and which were needed. Misunderstandings and strong feelings were not avoided, but, finally, a shared view was found: there could not be just one product API or one customer API. Project management should be rethought. The ways projects were launched, managed, budgeted, and resourced, and how their architectural solutions were made, should undergo reevaluation.

Teams were created to build grocery store APIs and ones that concentrated on hardware store APIs. Some focused in creating APIs for analytics and machine learning, especially product recommendations and other personalized services. Several teams were created to focus on customer loyalty programs. Different countries and industries required their own APIs: Finns, Swedes, and Russians – not to mention the Norwegians – may fit in the same sauna but not necessarily in the same API.

Whenever a new team was created around API or started to actively use the APIs provided by other teams, new discussion groups were created on the existing team platform. In half a year's time, two teams had increased to at least 30. One of the most compelling changes was that the "traditional" ERP teams and even the business unit representatives had been introduced to the discussion channels due to API development.

Several teams, other than those that directly developed APIs in the cloud environments, migrated to more agile methods with API development. In a top-priority project with a tight schedule, this was key, as the API team wanted test data and test cases during the first sprint. The project was originally designed with the traditional method, where all kind of testing would only take place at the end. Starting API testing at an early stage proved to be one of the success factors behind the project, enabling the immediate possibility to detect whether the specifications had been enough or not, if the user interface plans were delayed in terms of performance, and whether the test data for the systems was challenging and finding suitable test cases, products, customers, and so on.

However, the biggest difference from previous projects was that many people from different companies, countries, and business and IT departments were able to first verify, with the help of APIs, that the functionality developed in the project so far met the acceptance criteria. Above all, the participants in the project were able to test, in small pieces, that all the separate parts and resources worked, the algorithms were correct, and that the data was correct – while also being compared to the background systems data and previous implementations. Above all, non-technical project members reported the experience of using and testing the APIs as "empowering." They got their hands on something useful, something that allowed them to try out the performance of the implementation early, and they were able to communicate confidently and directly with the developers.

The project also saw promising results from the API expert's point of view that usability, user interface design, and even business modeling could be done so that requirements and design were also viewed from an API perspective. We looked at how APIs could help us improve our customer experience or at least avoid the employment of user experience or business models that would cause heavy and complex implementations and problems in production.

Sometimes, during the development, requirements to develop very complex algorithms were encountered (for example, in logistics-related features). We were able to (and had to) discuss compromises with decision-makers in charge of the business models: Should we buy and use a third-party API, in which the algorithm is able to solve – from a programming point of view – a complex packaging algorithm? Would it be enough, from a functional point of view, to limit the number of goods to be ordered so that the problem could be solved by "normal" programming? In this project, we used many external APIs, partially customized commercial APIs, and APIs produced by internal and external teams.

One of the biggest challenges in making everything work was getting the data correct. To maintain a high level of data quality in turn required several key processes and parts of the organization, as well as the background system, to be reviewed and cleared. This is perhaps not the first thing that comes to mind when talking about APIs or API consulting. However, it is often the hardest and most important part. Usually, at this point, it becomes clear that certain data has been collected only for the internal use of one organizational unit. The employees and managers of the business unit do not necessarily feel that it is their job to be responsible for how the information is made available to others or how it is used elsewhere. What if the data that is being collected from the target area is not enough for others to use but needs to be enriched? Or what if the quality of the data is not enough for others to use?

Solving such challenges often requires changes to the organization and responsibilities, as well as rethinking the design of internal functions and the introduction of customer-oriented thinking and service logic into the work culture. Often, even that is not enough. In general, no one deliberately wants to be part of the problem, but if the area of responsibility is well defined and the workload is already 150%, then leadership, change management, and decision-making are required before any API is properly launched with the correct data and supporting processes.

This all requires the ability for the API development manager to act as a "human hub," that is, to connect people and convey information to different parties. When APIs are created and documentation becomes available, the situation becomes easier: developer teams and experts start to communicate directly with each other but with the help of a collaborative platform. Such a step is essential, because it's possible that two different external developers are communicating with each other directly regarding the API specifications.

The more "junior" the developer at each end of the conversation, the more likely it is that he or she will carry out the "spec" as it is and without questioning. This process may create APIs designed as if over a broken phone line. Therefore, one needs to anticipate the optimal processes and communication and physical presence, at least when new APIs are planned or undergo major changes. When APIs with well-designed specifications and examples are used, it is often not necessary to have loads of meetings or documentation; all one needs is a link to the developer portal and a tip about which API to use. After that, communication proceeds mostly by asking specific questions, requesting new features, or reporting bugs.

No APIs Without Agile Methods

At present, it is trendy to implement a microservices architecture (architecture based on independent services and offering only a very limited functionality), which is based on the spirit of service-oriented architecture (SOA). One would hope that the same thing would not happen with the microservice, and especially the API architecture, as occurred with the service-oriented architecture: in most cases, it was considered merely a technical matter. This was proven by the 2009 SOA Manifesto, which aimed to correct these perceptions. Importantly, half of the manifesto deals with business and organizational aspects ***(highlighted with italics):***

1. ***Respect the social and power structure of the organization.***
2. ***Recognize that SOA ultimately demands change on many levels.***
3. ***The scope of SOA adoption can vary. Keep efforts manageable and within meaningful boundaries.***
4. ***Products and standards alone will neither give you SOA nor apply the service-orientation paradigm for you.***
5. SOA can be realized through a variety of technologies and standards.

6. Establish a uniform set of enterprise standards and policies based on industry, de facto, and community standards.
7. Pursue uniformity on the outside while allowing diversity on the inside.
8. ***Identify services through collaboration with business and technology stakeholders.***
9. Maximize service usage by considering the current and future scope of utilization.
10. ***Verify that services satisfy business requirements and goals.***
11. ***Evolve services and their organization in response to real use.***
12. Separate the different aspects of a system that change at different rates.
13. Reduce implicit dependencies and publish all external dependencies to increase robustness and reduce the impact of change.
14. At every level of abstraction, organize each service around a cohesive and manageable unit of functionality.

Although the manifesto was written over 10 years ago and the world has shifted in the direction of microservice architecture and APIs, the requirements of the manifesto continue to apply.

Experts who woke up to the API economy in Finland saw the same challenges in API development as they did in SOA. As a result, at the initiative of Jarkko Moilanen, they developed an *API Manifesto*[118] in 2015. More than technical aspects, the Manifesto emphasizes collaboration, the service strategy, and the culture of continuous development and co-development:

1. Serve digitally with the APIs.

2. Favor transparency.

3. Make the deployment as easy as possible.

4. Measure, learn from feedback, and iterate.

5. Collaborate with others.

6. Implement consistently.

7. Create APIs that serve a purpose.

While some points within the SOA manifesto overlap, one reaps the most benefits in the API economy by following a combination.

However, both manifestos were written at a time when the main use-cases for APIs were related to retrieving, creating, updating, and maintaining business information. The rate of change and the opportunities in both technology and business have increased over the last ten years. Attempts have been made to address these requirements with, e.g., Lean methods, Teal organizations, DevOps, and through the Agile Manifesto[119].

Agile Manifesto for Software Development

We are uncovering better ways of developing

software by doing it and helping others do it.

Through this work we have come to value:

Individuals and interactions over processes and tools

Working software over comprehensive documentation

Customer collaboration over contract negotiation

Responding to change over following a plan

That is, while there is value in the items on

the right, we value the items on the left more.

Agile methods are still "coming soon" in some companies and public-sector organizations. I have personally experienced in my work the truthfulness of the above manifestos. Therefore, I cannot stress enough that API architecture cannot be developed without agile methods. It is advisable to be prepared for many changes in how organizations and their internal teams work and network.

Summary

An API is not the same as an integration.

An API's ability to change an organization is two-sided.

APIs accelerate the transfer of knowledge and innovation from outside the organization to the inside.

API users make up an external community that can be used to create new ideas and reflect your own knowledge and competence needs.

APIs eliminate silos, improve communication, and change work culture.

APIs do not just change how IT, software development, or product development work; they also change the way an organization acquires and manages its services and how it handles budgeting, management, and outsourcing of services and resources.

12 ENCOUNTERS ON CANVAS

Marjukka Niinioja

"Feelings, nothing more than feelings..." The song is older than me, but for some reason, it hits the nerve and always plays in my head whenever I start creating an API strategy with a new client. I offer this warning beforehand that in this chapter I deal with the emotions raised by APIs and API development. Emotions and past perceptions of interfaces seem to be the greatest barrier an organization needs to overcome on its path to API development.

There are a few different feelings at play with a new customer. Some are usually somewhat aware of APIs, some of them are "integration people," and some are convinced of their own API ignorance. However, most believe that APIs are a matter for IT personnel and that IT specialists and software developers make decisions about API issues and know enough about the business's needs.

Some architects experience despair, loneliness, and stress due to ongoing encounters and endless meetings with business stakeholders. These poor architects must make an infinite number of slide decks, architectural designs, and reports, and in the worst-case scenario, nothing really changes. The common understanding behind such a scenario is that the people working on the business side do not understand technology and the developers don't know the business nor listen to requirements. Sometimes, it is not even possible to hire or contract developers, because time is spent in endless specification or procurement meetings.

There are, of course, positive feelings involved, which may lead to equally challenging situations: it may be that the word in the corridors says APIs are the one thing everyone has to have now. And yet there is no real understanding of what an API is and especially not who should be involved, what preparations should take place, and where these preparations should start. There is plenty of enthusiasm to go around but not much more!

Sometimes, software developers are hard-at-work creating APIs, but their intentions fall on barren ground. No one around them understands what it is all about (as seen in the previous chapter on the experiences of developers interviewed by Aitamurto and Lewis). Sometimes, the API was created several years earlier, but nobody really knows whether it was done well, why it is not being used enough, or how APIs should be done now. Occasionally, APIs abound but getting access to them is like trying to break into a bank vault: the documentation is lost, or no one is responsible for managing API support or has the power to decide which API to grant access to. The confusion makes the organization run in circles and gets teams to squabble.

These emotions towards APIs are alleviated by the API Canvas, which charts the encounters of all API-related entities' stakeholders. The API Canvas was introduced by 3Scale at APIdays Paris 2015. The audience was intrigued, but a single Canvas did not provide enough direction for understanding why it would be useful and what problem it would solve. Essentially, it was an API version of the Business Model Canvas. Jarkko Moilanen later blogged about the API Canvas on the NordicAPIs blog, but even that didn't help proliferate the idea of the canvas spread. Most likely, the readership – mostly composed of developers – had not yet embraced the business dimension of the APIs or couldn't fill the canvas alone or connect it to their API development process.

Previously, I started developing a new API with a team: I first went through the needs for the new API with the account managers and sales or customer service department, identifying what new customer segments, connectors, plugins, productized integrations, or user interfaces we could create if we had a specific API, as well as how much more revenue could we generate. Often, the need came directly from an existing customer with clear business potential, making it possible to assess whether the case was critical and whether it offered a new business potential or market value. Based on this assessment, we compared the estimated time, cost, and efforts required to develop the API. However, the process was not of a definitive nature, so this pondering and ensuing discussion might not have been conveyed to the team developing the API, even though I often tried to ensure their presence.

I ran into a new problem while moving away from developing commercial products toward developing internal APIs in support of new services and improving internal operations. The business need for an API was assessed only in terms of the development costs involved; the benefits were indirectly evaluated. Developers were often not involved because they were ordered to implement a solution that had already been decided on.

From the API developer's point of view, the design of an API therefore always started when the business decisions had already been made. Or, there existed only an earlier design decision made by the architects, without a business impact assessment – and this was the worse option.

Where to find the clues for API development? "Let's start with the customer journey and the value proposition," I say to the attendees at the start of a workshop. At this point, I'm usually confronted by blank stares, confused expressions, and deep thinking. Often, the attendees already have a certain API in mind, such as searching for the customer's basic information. When I ask why it is needed and what process or customer journey it is associated with, I get a confounded response:

"Well, you can use it anywhere, so what do you mean?"

"It will all become clear," I promise them. "Now, let's take a moment to figure out what someone would actually use this customer search for. It helps us focus on the right problems and to see the whole. Trust the process!"

In most cases, we get to move on from this stage. With some digging around, guesswork, and most often industry knowledge, one will locate the actual performed process and service that is to be developed further with the Canvas. If only technical specialists are present, the consultant will have to use all of her industry knowledge to get things moving forward from this point. That is why business representatives really should be present.

We will break down the customer journey and consider what benefits would be on offer for the application developers if the functionality were available through APIs. It is relevant to study the subject through the eyes of the API consumer, not the provider. In the same way, consider what obstacles or disadvantages API consumers might have when trying to use the available API.

These steps are intended to help one decide on the API product features desired by the API consumers and to help avoid or overcome the challenges (a.k.a. the pains, as described in chapter 2.) Next, we need to consider which APIs and other services could implement the listed features. This creates an API value proposition, initially for one group of API consumers.

From a Value Proposition to the Business Model

Next, the business model canvas is used to determine for which other segments the same value proposition would be relevant and how the API for these customer segments should be offered, communicated, marketed, and supported. All of this is done to make the API as effective as possible with minimum effort and maximum business benefits, such as:

- Increase of sales either through fees or volume growth
- Cost savings
- Increase in customer loyalty
- Innovative designs
- Increase of investments in startups

On the other side of the business model canvas, one needs to consider existing resources that would help develop the API so that it implements the intended value proposition. There one should list all the actions to be taken to fulfill the value proposition and the partners with whom these actions are taken. This creates the basis for the API's budget. One should consider development, marketing, communication, maintenance, and other costs.

As a result of carefully completing the Canvas, one will come to understand the profitability of the API; for example, the planned API would cost a company 50,000€ but would generate 1,000,000€ in revenue and result in 15,000€ in savings per year. The business case for creating such an API (or not) is made visible. It is advisable to use the canvases specifically for ideation and quick comparison of different options, as they render the whole picture visible. The main benefit is the discussion of IT costs and sales budgets in same meeting or at least connecting them together.

Tried and Tested

While working at Digia Plc, I developed an API development process and method, APIOps Cycles[120], which was consequently published under a Creative Commons license for public use. When I first led the Canvas workshop for a client, I was unsure. The idea was founded on solid theoretical arguments; however, I was afraid that the tools for service designers and business developers would seem too lightweight and flimsy for engineers.

I've witnessed how training sessions, workshops, and client meetings generate an enthusiastic, idea-rich, and collaborative atmosphere from which participants leave feeling empowered. Some of them say, "These APIs are actually not so complicated." Often architects are among the most enthusiastic, saying, "I finally got the tools to collaborate with others, so I don't need to do everything myself."

The use of the canvases and API development method has reminded me why I chose to study education first and foremost instead of computer science. It is a wonderful feeling to help people make sense of a new and difficult issue and to help them acquire the tools necessary for assisting their team in changing their work methods concretely.

Hopefully, you will also be able to experience positive encounters around the canvas. However, it's just the beginning!

Summary

One of the customers was convinced that he had "no use for slide decks," adding, "no system documentation can be documented with slides, especially something that looks like a coloring book. You can't store architecture that way."

It is true that slides are not the most convenient format for maintenance documentation. But it is not the purpose of these canvases, but to:

1) Act as tools for collaboration, communication and ideation.

2) Provide tools for cooperation and a common language for people from different backgrounds.

3) Help the business become interested in something that is essentially a piece of technology, but which is also a key part of the business model: how open the company culture is, who owns the customer experience,

which partners the company is working with, and whose resources are used.

4) Provide IT management with better visibility for business needs and tools to guide business to take advantage of technology.

5) Bring revenue and other business benefits into the conversation instead of costs, so that the "business case" can be created.

13 START BY EXPERIMENTING LIGHTLY

Mika Honkanen

This chapter introduces the stages of API development. In addition, we explain how to use the API interface description to begin lightly by gathering and reviewing comments from potential users and other parties before a single line is coded. Before implementing, it is crucial to make sure that API is really needed and that it meets your business needs.

For the development of a new API, one should take advantage of a quick trial. The key is to understand the value to be delivered to the customer. The Open API definition allows one to quickly iterate the functionality of API. So far, everything can be done without any programming skills. From the Open API definition, one can directly create stacks of different programming languages and sometimes software development packages, or SDKs, which can then be linked to interface data or functional logic. However, an automatically created software development package may need to be patched, whereas a manual creation process requires some human resources.

In the case of sensitive data, the API can first be tested with test data. After that, sufficient data security is built, the strength of which depends on the data and the API operating environment. Programming is only required for connecting an API to the correct data or for the implementation of functional API; everything else can be created quite quickly, automatically, and transparently in a programming language, platform, and application. The functionality of API can be scaled up, so start with a small and simple set.

Figure Out the Big Picture

Typically, an API's lifecycle is comprised of four stages:

1. Identification of need
2. Development and testing
3. Production
4. Disposal

In practice, stages 1 through 3 will, in part, be performed simultaneously. Designing a new interface should be guided by value creation. The goal of agile development is to produce value for the user/customer as much as possible, as quickly as possible.

When thinking about value, one can find a good reference point by comparing one's own value proposition with other APIs. Take the examples of Twilio[121], Stripe[122], GitHub[123], or SendGrid[124]: it is worth discussing with customers and striving comprehensively to understand their customer experience. One should actively try to imagine how to add value for customers. Comprehensive customer experience management means that all service, support, and interaction are part of the API product and offering.[125] A holistic approach is much more difficult to sell than a faster, cheaper, or more durable API product.

At the first stage, while gathering the customer needs and creating the rough design of the product, one can utilize, for example, user stories and agile development. The user story is a brief and simple description from the perspective of the API, and a good user story clearly explains who, what, and why. The writing of these is done by everyone after a small exercise. They are often written on post-it notes, which can be attached to the wall and organized in order of priority. User stories are often written at different levels of accuracy; one user story may contain a lot of functionality, for example. At this stage, it is not yet the goal to understand the structure of the API but rather to understand the need. The three most important things to consider here are:

1. How does API create value?
2. Who are the customers, and how do they find API?
3. How will the API be used and how will the API serve customers?

A user story including many functionalities is considered "epic." It can also be understood as a collection of user stories. An epic related to APIs could be, "I want to manage my personal information through interfaces." The epic is split into smaller user stories as part of the design process, and they can be large in number, depending on the epic.

User stories can be refined in at least two ways: either by splitting large stories into multiple smaller ones or by adding preconditions for stories to guide their creation. In general, it is not advisable to put too much functionality into one interface. To facilitate adoption, application developers prefer simple interfaces. With user stories and various methods of prototyping, one can quickly try different options for API functionality. At this point, it does not matter if the idea does not scale, as that can be addressed later.

One notable aspect of user stories is that the API will be defined from the user perspective and not from the provider perspective. The weakness of the user stories, on the other hand, is that they do not adequately address non-functional requirements.

Minimum Value-adding Product

When developing a new API, start by experiment quickly. An ongoing discussion is currently underway about the length of API lifecycles, and at this point APIs are being developed using agile software development methods. In addition, the needs and aspirations of application developers and the business environment are constantly changing.

In the first stage, there is no need to produce any code but only to try the logic – that is, what kind of request to send the API and what the API answers. Prototyping is cheap and very quick as compared to actual implementation. One's imagination is the only limit to how an API can be simulated without buying or programming a tool. Even pieces of paper can be used to simulate people and workflows in information systems.

Next, the idea of an interface can be tested with the Design-First approach by creating an Open API description. Open API describes the properties and functionality of API, which follows the RESTful software architecture in a consistent manner: it describes the structure of API and provides functions. The description can also be used to automatically create code templates for different programming languages. The Open API definition can be created in collaboration with application developers.

When designing an interface, its data model is often overlooked. The focus tends to be only on technical design, and the information architecture is not considered. In general, the public administrators' interfaces do not have properly described data models, and the semantic interoperability of the information is hardly thought-out. However, the Open API description alone does not sufficiently inform the interface model. It also leaves a lot of freedom to design the entire API. That's why style guides are needed, which we discuss in chapter 14.

"Mocking" (providing a virtual backend for the API) makes it possible to develop and respond to API calls at an early stage. For example, Dropbox has benefited from "mocking" in Dropbox API Explorer, and shortly thereafter, Amazon announced its own mock integration into its API management product. In this phase, the goal is to spend as little money and time as possible on producing the prototype of an API and to focus on testing and developing the idea.

The Minimum Viable Product (MVP)[126] is a product with just enough features to satisfy early customers and to provide feedback for future product development. The term was coined by Frank Robinson in 2001, but it became widely known by Eric Ries in his book *Lean Startup*. MVP aims to target groups of early adopters. As early as 1962, Everett Rogers introduced five user groups in his book *Diffusion of Innovations*. (User groups were discussed in more detail in chapter 10.)

With the help of MVP, feedback is provided by the first customers for further development of the API. If the API would have been developed directly, the cost of development would rise and the risk of product failure would increase; in this case, product development would be guided by an assumption of what customers need instead of hearing it from the customers themselves. The best information is available from its source, that is, the customer his- or herself, and the best way for the customer to answer questions is to try the (MVP) product.

The Open API definition is a reference framework and a way to describe an interface based on REST architecture. It is a machine-readable definition that illustrates, produces, consumes, and visualizes the interface structure. Previously, Open API was called Swagger. In 2015, a new organization called Open API Initiative was established under the Linux Foundation to develop an Open API definition. The organization includes, among others, IBM, Google, eBay, Microsoft, MuleSoft, Oracle (Apiary), PayPal, Salesforce, SAP, and 3Scale. The Open API definition is independent of the programming language. It offers its own ecosystem for the various tools that can automatically create documentation, thus considerably speeding up the building of an API. At the same time, security and quality remain high. Regardless of whether the API is designed for external or internal use, it needs to be designed the *right* way. With the Open API reference frame, both the source code and the documentation are updated simultaneously.

The interface MVP is a specification with sample invitations and responses. It can be implemented with the Open API specification and expanded with examples and schemata depending on the media type. The strength of the Open API definition is its open source tools.

From these, the Swagger Editor can design, describe, and document an API description. Descriptions are created in either JSON or YAML data formats. The Swagger Codegen tool creates an interface code template for the Open API description. The Swagger UI tool enables API to test with a web browser in a visual format and works with all browsers. The Swagger Inspector tool enables testing of the API as well as the creation of the Open API definition based on the tests.

Innovators, one of the user groups presented in Rogers' study, are capable of experimenting with new things, can accept more incompleteness of a product, and will provide feedback to aid further development. With interfaces, a small group of customers can be selected to test the new version. It is worth telling them at this stage that this is a new implementation. The goal is to validate the MVP with as little effort as possible. Validated learning refers to a process in which assumptions are tested in practice, with the aim of achieving real value-added information about the business environment and its future development. At the interface, one can test whether customers are willing to pay for or even use it; for example, if application developers need an interface to reliably send text messages to customers.

MVP aims to:

1. Test your product-related assumptions with minimum resources
2. Accelerate learning

3. Minimize time spent before introducing the product to the market
4. Bring customers to your product as quickly as possible
5. Create ideas for other products

One might want to try several ideas and be prepared to pivot if they do not work. At this point, going another direction won't cost much and changes are easy to implement. Experimenting helps to evaluate, predict, understand, control, and improve the software development product and process.[127]

Stabilize the Facade

When building the elements of the interface, incorrect changes can lead to a breakdown of their functionality. More functionalities can be added, but the modification of existing ones violates the applications on which they are built. Therefore, it is important to consolidate and standardize the structure to the extent that it affects the applications built on the interface. New features can be introduced later by upgrading the interface or building new interfaces.[128] At this point, one is striving for an interface structure that responds well to customer needs. After that, the structure (facade) should be standardized so that customers of the interface can concentrate on utilizing it. At this stage, the technical implementation of the machine operating under the interface may still be an MVP.

Establishing a facade means that the Open API definition is complete and published, and based on that documentation, client source code templates and server source code templates are created. The Open API specification can automatically create client- and server-source code templates for over 30 different programming languages. The bases are not ready-made code as such, but they provide the programmer the bases to supplement their own code.

It is good to inform the API consumers in advance about plans to develop and upgrade an interface. For example: "This version is supported for the next three years and new versions will appear every nine months."

New features can be brought to the interface, but often a good interface is quite simple to use and understand. One should also use the interface oneself so that the organization understands the perspective of the customer when interacting with the interface.

Once Interface Experiments are Complete, Infrastructure Experimentation Begins

When the product implementation of an API has been taken far enough, the interface begins to quickly gain more customers. At this point, it needs to be scaled. Scaling refers to the process of responding to growing customer needs and increasing the capacity of the interface. Scalability should be undertaken with baby steps. An effective strategy is to focus on the worst bottlenecks in performance, then rectify them. Behind an API facade, one can change everything without revealing it elsewhere. For instance, eBay architecture is operating with its fifth generation. First, it was programmed in the Perl programming language, then in the C ++ programming language, then in Java, and now is implemented as microservices.

The following table shows the execution times of eBay, Twitter, and Amazon.

Examples of API code rewrites:[129]

Service	1st generation	2nd generation	3rd generation	4th generation
eBay	Perl	C++	Java	Microservices
Twitter	Rails	JS / Rails / Scala	Microservices	

Amazon	Perl	C++	Java / Scala	Microservices

First, one should stop pursuing perfection in API architecture. Even the world's largest software houses are constantly changing the source code of their services in small chunks. The best software code one can possibly produce now will last only a few years. Microservices are again being written regularly. For example, Google employs 25,000 software developers committing 45,000 changes to its software every day. All software code on Google provides and uses APIs. Google has produced two billion lines of code to implement its services:[130] new code is produced constantly, and 15 million lines of the existing code is edited every week.

Plan the Lifecycle Before Publishing

In practice, technical debts are inherent to all software products. Business needs are changing, and technologies are evolving. The lifecycle of an interfaces ends with the use of controlled removal, and the entire lifecycle should be considered at the publication stage. As well, customers should be informed about key stages of interface development. The disposal should be done in a controlled manner, and it is advisable to inform customers well in advance, as they must be afforded sufficient time to update their own software to take advantage of newer versions of the interface or other replacement products.

Even the slightest uncertainty about the length of an API's lifecycle will effectively prevent its adoption. Therefore, it is advisable to strongly consider the lifecycle-frame and then communicate openly during the planning phase. For how long is the API provider prepared to support and provide the product?

In the case of multiple interfaces, the question of their mutual unity and similarities will arise. How does one build API families – all sharing similar characteristics? This is the core of the next chapter, which discusses the API design guide for API development and behavior.

Summary

Start with the Open API specification. Perform "user research"; that is, collect feedback from potential API users before you start to code.

By using standards such as the Open API specification to get the documentation done easily, one can publish the API to the API management tool.

It is worthwhile to pay attention to data models (schemas, connection request, and response) and describe them as part of the API specification.

For more information on how to design an API specification, see chapter 14.

The value and value proposition are discussed in more detail in chapter 2.

14 STYLE ABOVE CODE – API DESIGN GUIDE

Jarkko Moilanen

An API design guide steers API development by creating conditions for maintained interfaces and lifecycles. A unified standards-based style for an API family creates a professional image, increases predictability, saves development costs, speeds up API development, and facilitates deployment, thus increasing API usage. The design guide is not a separate "island" but at best is a tool for mediating the relationship between the various parties in the API development process.

Standard Interfaces

Digital service development has long been accustomed to graphical guidelines that define the boundary conditions for using a logo, such as protection zones, colors, and fonts.[131] APIs are no exception. An API design guide – a style guide – is also made for interfaces. Large, successful companies such as Google, Microsoft, and Kesko have opened up their API style guide for everyone. The guide does not take a stand on programming language but lays out boundary conditions for design and implementation in the same way graphical guidelines do when using a company logo. In short, an API style guide is a means of standardizing API design, development, and style.

When considering the style of an API, one may first think of the unity and readability of the code. Although the API style certainly affects and therefore guides everything else, the effect and purpose of the style guide is much wider. For the REST API, the style guide is of great importance, because REST is an architectural style[132], not a standard, and thus allows plenty of room for maneuvering. The commonly used Open API specification generates a framework for API description but leaves details such as error handling and parameter naming practices to the responsibility of the developer.

It is said that the devil lives in the details. The central task of the API design guide is to standardize the REST APIs for one's organization, regardless of whether they are internal or external. Typically, the REST API style guide[133] includes at least the following:

- Policies for naming endpoints and parameters
- Versioning (new version numbers are generally assigned in increasing order and correspond to new developments in the software; in this case, also the interface description)
- Error handling
- Security practices (authentication/access control)
- Data models (standards used)
- Methods used (CRUD) and their possible responses in different situations.

The best way to start with API style guides and the good practices that can be learned through them is to familiarize yourself with existing versions. One can get acquainted with several company style guides through API Stylebook[134]. However, one should take care to not blindly copy from the existing examples, as they may contain incorrect or only partially functional solutions.

Crafting a style guide is worthwhile, because the style affects the entire lifecycle of the API. It facilitates and speeds up the process, provides the conditions for a unified developer experience, lessens the learning curve, reduces the workload of the API developer[135], and promotes code maintainability.

A style guide is part of an API's governance, which differs from an API's technical management, (further discussed in chapter 18), which refers to API management as a process and practice in a broader sense. API management includes lifecycle, deployment, and technical management of the use and applicable practices.[136] Policies are often written as guides, just like the API Stylebook. The following examples illustrate how the API style guide direct the development of both new and existing APIs to be versioned.

The Role of the API Design Guide in API Development

Share Openly

An API style guide should not be hidden in an intranet or anywhere else within a system. Instead, the style guide should be publicly available. Transparency has its advantages: subcontractors may, without a separate request, read the same instruction when implementing the API and see how different parts of the API should be built for the end-result to be aligned with the needs of other parties implementing the same API or API family.

In addition, through openness, the company can garner feedback from a broad community about its API style guide and thus find ways to improve its own API package to become more developer-friendly and consistent with ever-changing industry practices. The style guide is therefore not a "write once" document; it also requires updating. Considering the wide-ranging effects of the style guide, updates should be done with care and control. Usually, the style guide is written before the broader API production, precisely because of its influence on and guidance throughout the process. Once the style guide has been created, it should be widely made available and communicated to all parties and used in the API review process.

Controlled Versioning

Changes to an existing API must always consider the effects on applications that already use it. At worst, radical alteration of an existing function causes backward incompatibility and affects hundreds or thousands of applications (depending on the popularity of your API). Generally, at this point, versioning is done, and the previous version is left unchanged. Examples of backward-breaking changes include removing a parameter from an API call, making an optional parameter mandatory, deprecating (discontinuing to provide) an API call, or changing data types in parameters or response patterns.[137] Because the effects of the changes may be severe, the API style guide usually determines, with reasonable precision, which changes will fire the versioning process.

The "Design-first" Approach is Often Worthwhile

The API design guide is important when applying the design-first principle in the development of an API. In this case, the design of the API is complete before the actual functionality is implemented. Typically, the result of the design is a machine-readable description[138] of the functionality, endpoints, parameters, and used data models. The API design defines the API before the coders are free to implement logic and integrations to backend systems.

Another option is the "Code-First" approach, in which the API is implemented based on the business needs defined, for example, by the API Model Canvas. The machine-readable description is then generated programmatically from the code and the comments it contains.

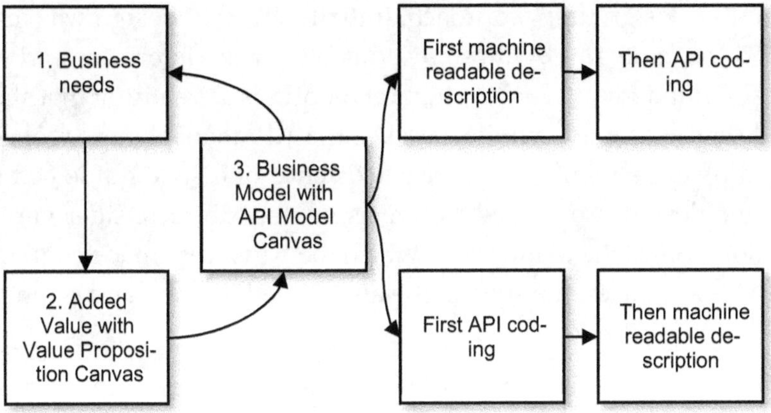

Figure 11 API development deriving from business reasons might proceed code or design first

In addition, hybrid forms, in which approaches are combined, are a possibility. In this case, the design may be made first and validated by external API consumers. Next, the API is implemented and, finally, as part of the publishing process, parts of the code are drawn into the documentation while the machine-readable description produced in the design phase is partly reused. In this case, however, there is a risk that the implementation does not always correspond to the initial formatting of the API. Such risk can be mitigated by performing tests against the machine-readable description while implementation proceeds.

The Design Guide Evolves Through Indirect Feedback

One example of a hybrid model is the development of the REST APIs contained in APInf Oy's API management solution, whose API Design guide and API development process I led in 2017.[139] At that time, the reason for choosing a hybrid model was the architecture of the platform.

Although a hybrid model was in use, it did not differ ostensibly from the "design first" approach. Initially, the API design was made within the company by those responsible for the interfaces and was first provided for internal evaluation for others. Already, at that stage, the design was made public, because the API management tool contained lifecycle management. The existence of a style guide accelerated the design process, as there was no need to reconsider various solutions. Since the platform for which the APIs were made contained multiple interfaces, the style guide also served to unify and standardize.

The management of the API machine-readable description based on Open API specification was located in the same source code repository as other parts of the system (GitHub), and the API management retrieved the API description, if necessary, instead of being manually loaded into the API portal. This automation saved time and was part of the continuous integration process.

After internal evaluation and corrections (a few rounds), a message was sent to trusted external API consumers who'd been gathered through API community meetings. These consumers included the early adopters of the Rogers model described in chapter 10. They were able to read the API documentation and comment on API formatting directly through API management. All comments became public by default.

Within a few weeks – after enough feedback had been submitted – corrections were made to the design of the API, and then it was implemented. At the same time, the API lifecycle status in the API management was changed to "development" mode, at which point the API style guide became worth its weight in gold, as API implementers were located around the globe: one in Brazil, one in India and the third in Finland. The style guide directed the work of the API developers and accelerated implementation, as dialogue between the implementers (among other things) was omitted. Once the implementation was completed and tested, the same machine-readable description was used in production.

As well, the API design guide was located in the same code management system as the codes and API machine-readable descriptions. When the team found a pattern emerging in the feedback, which was contrary to the style guide, it was added to the code management system. Changes to the style guide were evaluated, and if it was a small change, it was incorporated immediately. In most cases, the changes were related to information to be written for the API consumers and not to code implementation. Correspondingly, the developer responsible for the development of the APIs made requests for changes to existing interfaces. In the early stages, the style guide changed often until it began to find its form through experience.

Evaluate and Validate API Design

API design inspection should be considered on at least two levels: technical validation against specification and logical user evaluation. By employing early adopters in evaluation and review, you avoid the most common mistakes and thus learn more and faster. Of course, if you use the Open API specification in the API description, the result must be technically validated to ensure design description conformity with the applied standards. If the description is not technically valid, it is often not possible to use it for generating code or SDK packets, for example. Equally, a technically flawed description prevents its use in generating API consumer-oriented documentation.

An API style guide naturally guides the work of the API designer. It is not advisable to design APIs in an ivory tower isolated from end-users (API consumers). By focusing on the API design first, and by making it available to third parties for "proofreading," one avoids costly mistakes. The ideal audience for validating the first drafts of the API design are the early adopters. At best, their feedback will help one avoid design choices unlikely to appeal to the API consumers. In addition, the feedback highlights potential shortcomings in logic and operations, as well as documentation. Google systematically uses external evaluators in the development of its APIs.[140] Based on the feedback received, the formatting of the API is modified and only then implemented at code-level.

Formulate, Test, Evaluate

An API style guide will speed up and facilitate the testing and writing of test cases (partially automatically generated). Tests can be written before code-level implementation if the API design is in progress. Often, the authoring of tests, writing of some code experiments against formatting, and the design itself go hand in hand.

Why should one also write test code? By experimenting with the code, one can determine whether the API is efficient and easily consumed in the operations planned for it and whether it corresponds to use cases. The test codes can be used as part of API documentation, because API users are application developers, and the most natural "documentation" for them is the code example. The code examples are exactly what the users are expecting.[141] In other words, try to picture the activities of the API through the eyes its consumer.

At this point, one can consider using a prototype API (mockup) that can be generated from a machine-readable API description. At the same time, when the API design is given to a third party for evaluation, one can (and should) provide them with access to the API prototype. The platform on which the design is made may also include the generation of an automatic mockup service.[142] (More about prototyping in chapter 13.)

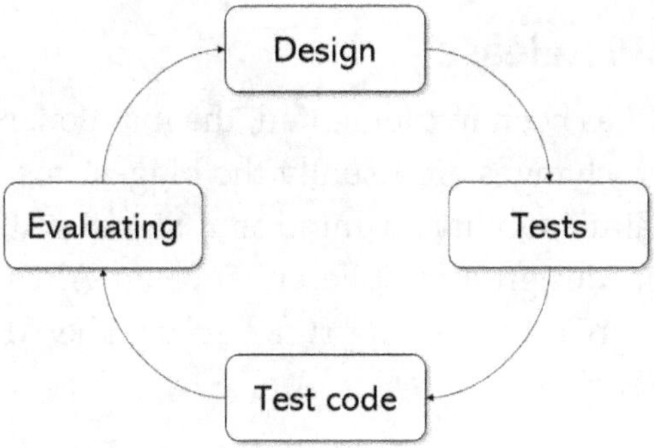

Figure 12 Cyclic API design process with different phases

Use Standards

Not everything is worth inventing yourself. Instead, de facto standards and practices in the field of API design can and often should be explored and implemented. For example, in data models, use of industry-standard solutions are advisable so the APIs will be familiar to the global user community, as the solution is built on a solid foundation and clarifies and speeds up development.

For example, most APIs include dates and times as either call parameters or content received in response to an API call. There are countless options for presenting a date, and the best way to standardize the date presentation for the entire API family is to define its format in one's API style guide. A good starting point is the inclusion of time zone information for elements that contain time references, because one never knows where the background systems, the API service, or the API users will be located. In addition, provide an example in the API documentation. Google, for example, has set the date in its own API style guide to always be in ISO 8601 format.

After the API Release

After the API has been implemented, the maintenance phase begins, which is when changes are usually the biggest cost item. Designing with code maintainability in mind is a significant way to manage costs. Uniform design and style enhance an API's maintainability. The impact is great in the long run, because the APIs are in use for years before retiring.

Among other things, the consumption of APIs is proven to be hampered by inadequate API documentation, code examples of how to utilize the API, and a lack of use case descriptions.[143] When studying the interfaces of large companies, their style guides are the ideal source of key information. With such a guide, the API consumer can, from one source, quickly and easily get their hands on the overall design principles for the company's interfaces. Thus, in addition to directing subcontractors and in-house developers, the open API style guide serves the developer network.

Summary

A unified standards-based style across the API family creates a professional image, enhances predictability, saves development costs, speeds up API development, facilitates deployment, and thus increases API usage.

The central task of the style guide is to standardize the design, development, and behavior of the organization's REST APIs, regardless of whether the consumers are internal or external.

Use standards in the API description and data models.

Use third-party developers to evaluate the API design to avoid the worst mistakes and maximize the developer experience.

Explore existing public API design guides and publish your own before you start a broader API production.

15 AUDIT YOUR APIS

Marjukka Niinioja

Auditing refers to verification: Are all things related to form, style, content, and security being considered? The APIs you audit may be the ones you have just developed or the ones you are buying. Perhaps you've inherited an API from your predecessor. Possibly, you got the API as an add-on when you purchased a ready-made application. So, what is auditing needed for?

Auditing can be used to decide on the purchase of a single system or commodity containing APIs. Its purpose is to answer the question of whether the APIs are "good enough." Of course, it is worth selecting the audit criteria so that they do not aim for any objective general quality but expediency.

When an API is created or planned, there are many questions to keep in mind: Is the API good enough, can I publish the API to others, is it valid for publishing through the API management tool, and is it safe? Often, the people most concerned with these questions are the project manager, architect, integration expert, or other quality, delivery, budget, or maintenance managers.

Isn't it enough for a security testing company to do a security audit on the API? What's so unique about this API stuff? Isn't a security audit enough? What else should be checked?

Security or Compliance?

API auditing may be inadequate if it is only an API security audit. Security audits are often performed based on general security criteria and involve a lot of automated testing. Adequate information security auditing also includes human testing and analysis. However, testing depends on what the API provider and developers have been able to reveal about the purpose and use of an API, and what the security auditor is aware of and thus should suspect. For example, both the architect and auditor should know who the API's consumers will be and what privacy or other regulations the API falls under.

Without a formal checklist for the API, the person performing the security audit should be well-versed in the API world in order to be suspicious and demand certain features and design principles. For example, it is not advisable to put personal IDs in URL parameters, because they are logged. Logs, on the other hand, may easily end up outside the EU, in cloud services, or in the hands of service managers who are neither EU citizens nor even contracted with an EU-based company. Such a situation leads to illegalities involving the transfer of personal data from the EU. At such a point, it is no longer a security issue but a compliance issue, which is harder to check automatically.

The topic of sensitive data, like many other API security issues, is mentioned in an expertise-requiring, technical way in the Open Web Application Security Project's (OWASP) REST API checklist.[144] It is problematic if security challenges come up only when a valuable security expert has already been called on-site to test the API. What if problems are detected? You will then have to correct the implementation, possibly quite thoroughly, and repeat the audit. This results in additional costs and time. Wouldn't it be better for API developers and API product managers or others responsible for published APIs to be able to do a thorough audit during the design and development process?

Security design for the API may be a time-consuming and complicated process if, for example, identity management, authentication, or access management aren't yet solved or if they are not API-compliant.

These issues are discussed in more detail in chapter 20, but it is essential that each API contains the solutions required for its risk level.

The emerging API developers (and even the more experienced ones) post security-related challenges that cause some headaches; for example, SQL and JavaScript injections. "Injection" means that the API parameters are used to enter fragments of a database query or JavaScript, which is usually only used in the user interface code. A database query snippet may even cause the entire database to be deleted or all data found in the database to be included in the response without any access or other filtering. JavaScript in APIs, in turn, causes damage when the result returned by an API is directly loaded into an HTML page in the user interface and malicious JavaScript is downloaded to the user's browser.

These ailments are cured if the audit checklist (consider using the checklist template in APIOps Cycles[145]) reminds developers of the mantra, "Validate input, sanitize output." So, check the incoming input and clean up the output to be returned – always in this order. Validation also means changing the format of the parameters. At its simplest, it means numbers are numbers and text are text. There are no unsafe special characters or text snippets that the server software might interpret as a database query, for example. Such an interpretation could lead to erroneous action, an excess of information shown to users, or even removal of the entire database.

The API assumes that it has been given numbers as a value for a parameter. If the API is given special characters for input or 1 = 1 (meaning "restore all" in database queries), the API should say to the caller, "400 Bad Request." This answer means that the user has made a mistake, and the API request will not get through to the database.

The checklist should also include identifiers and their format. For example, the direct use of database ID numbers is often a bad idea. Users can guess them too easily or make unintentional errors, such as removing the wrong resource. A typical problem is, for example, the different perception of database and user interface developers as to what number is used to start a sequence of identifiers. In the database, a sequence of numbers often starts with 1, and in a JavaScript-enabled user interface, developers assume a sequence begins from 0. Take an API endpoint such as "/customers." If one enters the value 1 (the first customer) as a parameter (i.e., input) as such: "/customers /1," this means that we want to either "GET" the details of the first customer, update the record, or delete it, depending on the method being used.

Someone can easily make the mistake of thinking they are handling the second and not the first customer record in their code, depending on where their programming language thinks that numbers start in a sequence, either 1 or 0. For example, making an API that combines multiple background systems is challenging when using the database identifier (the number in sequence given by the database) directly. So, use a UUID or Universally Unique Identifier[146] to identify resources.

Usability Testing is Also Part of the API

In addition to minding the security, building an API requires many other wonderful tasks, too. There exist many specific methods, standards, and tools for testing the quality of a user interface, such as usability testing. An API is a user interface in the same way as one that contains fonts, colors, and buttons. An API also incorporates "design," meaning good, bad, or standard design. As with the web application interface, one must work with different browsers, follow the HTML5 standard, and define layout-related issues with CSS styles;

one needs to also design the interface of the API. Preferably, the design definition should be done using certain specifications, such as Open API, which has become the industry standard in recent years.

In the audit phase, one must check to see if the specification has been used, that it has been used correctly, and that the interface-specification-related files follow the standard of the selected specification and are validated correctly. Too often, the interface description is only written "because it has to be" or it is generated automatically from the code. Automated tests are often not written or run in accordance with interface descriptions. This leads to challenges for API documentation automation, API user tools, and API documentation to match the specification, not to mention how the API and its underlying code have been implemented.

When considering an API's demands and quality, it is also worth remembering the financial side. The quality, safety, and reliability of API must be proportional to its intended use. Some requirements may become unreasonably expensive. For example, an API made according to the OWASP criteria requires token-based authentication (see chapter 20 for more details), which is required when confidential information is passed on in the API or if the API is used on "unreliable" devices. Take a mobile application as an example, where it is easy to extract API keys from the code: an API that provides users with the same product or price information as is found on the company's public website and is mainly used in marketing applications does not necessarily require such a rigorous solution.

The application utilizing the API is also required to be fit for purpose and budget. For example, a marketing application that distributes banner ads to websites may not support complex identification methods or even complex API calls. Customizing the software available as a cloud service is either impossible or too expensive. It's worth thinking about which one will be more affordable: making the API lighter with identification and public information for marketing use or paying for customization. Often, for a large company, it is best to have a static file hand-picked from a suitable API for banner advertising and put it on the web server where the banner application retrieves the information. Identity management and authentication (IAM) services for APIs can be obtained as cloud services for a few euros but also as ready-made products. Of course, data protection requirements must be considered. Also, not all IAM services are suitable for API authentication needs. (This is further discussed in chapter 20.)

The idea of API auditing is that there is at least a common checklist for a team or buyers of APIs. In API development, it is essential that there is some list of "definition of done" typically used with agile development, at least one that must be thought-out and explained. Methods to ensure that those checklist items relevant to a specific API are also implemented. There are a lot of details that, new API developers may not realize or deem necessary.

The checklist is also needed because many API management solutions are quite demanding. For example, if using Open API mapping or schemes and examples, they must be implemented in accordance with the standard, otherwise they will not go through the publishing process or will only support a versioning method or certain authentication methods. The purpose of the checklist is therefore to remind one of things that are planned and to be clarified during the development phase or preferably at the design stage. The purpose of the checklist should not be to set best practices in stone for all APIs; the goal is to bring on suitably comprehensive guidelines to make the developers think about, discuss, and find the right solutions for this API (or why it would be wise to depart from the general principles).

Did You Buy or Inherit Your API?

It is also useful to have a checklist when you are purchasing an application providing APIs, a single API, or API development work. Then, of course, it is advisable to include the usual purchasing criteria in the checklist, such as how trustworthy the API provider is, where the data is stored and processed, what the terms of use are, pricing models and service level, and how information security and compliance are handled. The best idea is to live-test the checklist requirements before deciding to buy. Of course, if you are buying an easily interchangeable functionality offered by several different API vendors and the exchange doesn't require many lines of code, the situation is slightly different.

A checklist is also useful if you inherit an API from your predecessor, another vendor, or another team – or if you decide to take care of a mistreated or neglected API with your team, inheriting it from other teams or organizations after some organizational change. Then, with the help of the checklist, one can easily determine the current state, the amount of technical debt, and the development needs.

Another feasible way to have your own API instantly audited and assessed is to put your API in the hands of the developers about to consume it as early as possible, preferably before many lines of code have been produced. For example, you can experiment with your API by participating in a hackathon, where you will get feedback from many developers at once. One can do so even if only definitions and examples of data are available and not a fully working API.

At the point when the first working versions of the API are ready, it is worthwhile to crowdsource the testing, at least for a moment. Why not use crowdsourcing in later stages, too? Often, security-related "bug bounty" programs[147] and regular meetings with the developer community provide a solid opportunity to do so. Hackathons and developer meetings are also a good way to acquire new development ideas and identify promising recruits.

Summary

A checklist includes security (e.g., OWASP: Open Web Application Security) and compliance with standards and legal requirements. The list should also check that the API meets the design principles set in the style guide.

Remember to work according to purpose! Do not make your API too safe or compliant with all best practices if that results in a poorly suited API. Also, mind the budget.

A checklist can be used for both API development and API purchasing decisions. It is also useful when the person responsible for the API is replaced.

16 THE DEVELOPER EXPERIENCE IS THE NEW BLACK

Jarkko Moilanen

This chapter explains which interfaces developers are falling in love with and being shared with other users. In addition, consideration will be given to creating a winning situation using the understanding of the customer path and customer experience. The end-result is a developer experience that increases your API sales and strengthens the API community.

Interfaces to Fall in Love With

The developer experience is crucial. If it is not properly considered, the consumer selects another API (if there is one available). Modern application development is based on an increasing use of API. At the same time, the number of APIs has grown from hundreds to tens of thousands. It is no wonder, therefore, that the requirements for interfaces are increasing as competition intensifies.

A good developer experience enables quick first-time success, demonstrates further opportunities, is easy to deploy, and increases customer satisfaction. However, an optimal developer experience is not just an introduction or first touch; the ideal experience is created throughout the lifecycle of an API whenever the user receives support in different situations. In the battle of APIs, the game is lost if one API offers an experience enabling quick success, up-to-date and easy-to-access documentation, and support for problematic scenarios.

I have talked to hundreds of API developers and consumers about the developer experience, and it has become my special interest within the API economy, because I've worked as a liaison between developers and the business side.

For a long time, I was looking for a suitable example of Finnish-origin API with great developer experience. Developers in my network offered Stripe, but it is not Finnish, as the proposer immediately stated. The API quest involved longer discussions on Twitter, and finding a good example seemed impossible. Instead, one of Finland's most experienced developers of APIs, Viljami Kuosmanen, commented, "Oh, I haven't encountered any that I would remember. But you can ask me for examples of one million miserable SAP integrations :)."

Finally, the tone of the discussion went in a more positive direction when the Helsinki Region Transport (HSL) APIs were highlighted, especially their GraphQL API.[148] I've worked with HSL staff for some years and know that the developer experience is important to them.

How does the HSL API make the developer experience so enjoyable and fruitful? The answer from Timo Koola, who first mentioned the idea of on Twitter, contained both expected and surprising elements: "Documentation is, if not perfect, at such a good level. The API can be run with full data locally in Docker, and the live API can be played directly in the browser."[149]

Koola raised two important issues. First, the live API for direct scanning allows the developer to test API behavior without any installation or delay. The developer is not offered a demo but is granted direct access to the API and real data. This reduces the threshold for familiarization with the API and makes it possible for the API consumer to more deeply trust the API's potential. Second, HSL provides an easy, documented way to replicate the API in one's own environment. The reason the developer wants to do this is because interfering factors can be minimized, finding code errors is more efficient, and the developer has more freedoms to experiment.

Great developer experience includes API documentation, code examples to be copied, and use case descriptions. A lack of these has been proven to slow down the adoption of APIs.[150] HSL is not satisfied with this but has gone a step further by offering its full "dockerized" container of the API environment. Usually, API providers are satisfied with less than what HSL has created. Many of the developer interviews I have conducted have highlighted the need to create a copy of the API in one's own development environment, against which one can develop one's own application — which is what HSL's solution offers in a very rich data-rich format. A lighter solution is to provide developers with a machine-readable API description from which the developer can, with the help of the tools, generate API in his or her own development environment. In this case, the data used by API is often poor but robust enough for the purpose.

Attention has shifted from the features of the interface toward the developer, who is the primary customer of any API.[151] Petri Aukia spoke at the API Economy 101 seminar on Feb 6th, 2018 and highlighted the term B2D, Business to Developer marketing, where the software developer is not a servant but the whale everyone is trying to catch. HSL has understood the importance of B2D and has worked hard to get developers to fall in love with its interfaces.

At the same time, API providers need to understand the customer experience, i.e.: the journey to finding the API, the first encounter, and what happens after deployment. The customer experience can be divided into three consecutive stages: pre-acquisition, acquisition, and post-acquisition.[152]

Customer Journey as a Common Narrative

Before an API is introduced, various touchpoints happen in the life of the customer and their interaction with the service provider; likewise, this occurs after the deployment of the API, too. In most cases, this is called a customer journey.[153] Discussions with API users have highlighted two main ways to make first API contact. Sometimes, an API consumer is only given an API and is tasked with building the required functionality for the service being developed. Forcing the API down the developer's throat is a boring and straightforward path, and it will continue very predictably.

The second route, on the other hand, is more complex.

The API consumer is likely to search for a suitable API through the search engine – that's how he or she lands on the ProgrammableWeb site or ends up going directly to the company's developer center. Likewise, he may end up in a Stack Overflow conversation or Amazon Web Service catalog. More and more, the larger developer network is a source of information. Developers ask questions and share answers on Twitter, Facebook, or Slack channels.

It is essential to understand that the client's paths stems from multiple locations and with different tools, and that the paths cannot be controlled completely.[154] Sometimes, the choice of API takes place before the user has even seen API documentation or read alluring phrases and been teased by portals created by the marketing department. API consumers give credit to their peers and their recommendations.[155] Sites decorated with marketing language can easily create the impression that the API consumer must talk to an eager salesperson. That alone can be enough for them to seek out an alternative API.

Eventually, the consumer is directed to the API portal or the developer center. From there, the consumer must find the desired API and access it. In most cases, the user is still weighing a few APIs and has yet to make a choice. So, the "deal" is not necessarily closed yet.

At this point, it is essential to ensure that the potential customer understands the problem that the API will resolve. Immediately afterward, the user wants to try and see how the API works. Usually, a good solution is to offer a live environment where one can try out the different functionalities of the API. If the API experimentations require logging in, one should make sure that it does not become a barrier. Although the marketing department would like to know everything about the customer, one should minimize the customer's discomfort at this point.

In addition, a potential customer will likely want to know how the API is used and if it suits their purpose. A common way to avoid the conundrum posed by a paywall barrier is to offer a "freemium" plan or trial period. With this little trick, a potential customer might be hooked and more likely to become a paying customer. Don't make payments too difficult to understand but express them clearly and publicly. Nobody asks for pricing info by email unless absolutely compelled (i.e., rarely).

Next, the user wants to use the API within their own code. A common method is to provide copy-paste code examples of the basic API functionality. Code examples and proper documentation support each other and are, in the best cases, one and the same package. The examples provided in one programming language are a good start, and one should choose the most commonly used programming language of the API target group. Sometimes, one might stumble upon documentation where code examples are provided in several programming languages.[156] Before rushing into multi-language examples, one should remember that code examples must also be maintained when versioning and changing an API, unless examples are generated automatically.

If the user has been satisfied with his journey so far, a company is very likely to have found a new customer. Easy, isn't it? However, the client's path does not end once the API is deployed.

An API consumer wants to be apprised of forthcoming changes to or versions of the API. A window to the future of an API (road map) is of high interest to consumers. In addition, the reliability of the API is key to creating a more lasting customer relationship. Great documentation and code examples are not always able to answer all questions, and customer support therefore becomes essential.

A loyal API customer shares positive experience with other API consumers via blogs, social media, and presentations. A satisfied API consumer will become an ambassador for a company or brand; the earlier-mentioned Twitter discussion about the HSL interfaces is one example. Few APIs reach this level, but all should aim for such heights.

Developer Experience Is Not Just Technology

With the very general customer journey described above, it is easy to understand that the developer experience is not just a technological construct. Rather, the developer experience is part of the customer experience (CX), which is a broader entity or structure that includes social, cognitive, emotional, behavioral, and sensory elements.[157] When comparing how developer experience and customer experience are defined in research literature, similarities are easy to find.

According to one study, the developer experience is a complex concept. Experience is always individual. Developer experience involves a lot of learning and is therefore explained through cognitive (thinking and memory), conative (motivation), and effective (emotions and mood) learning theories. In addition, the technical and social environment has an impact on developer experience.[158] In short, the developer experience (DX) is a construct in the developer's head, including his or her perception of the development environment and a sense of his or her own work and its importance as part of the whole.

User experience (UX) is familiar to many. It can be used as a tool for understanding and explaining the developer experience. However, it should be noted that UX and DX are not the same thing. In the user experience, the focus is on the product and its use, while the focus of the developer experience is on product development. In other words, UX is a user-centered operating model, while DX is process-product-centered. And because DX is also influenced by social factors, understanding the developer community is crucial.

A Good Developer Experience Is the Sum of its Parts

A good starting point for understanding and crafting a developer experience is to think carefully about why an API exists, what problems it solves, and for which functions it needs to provide solutions. This has been the starting point for SOA architecture thinking.

Nowadays, attention has shifted more from the features of API to the developer who uses it. In other words, the focus has shifted to the customer (business to developer, B2D). Developer-centricity and what API-users feel are secondary if the API does not do what it is supposed to. Features and "feel" are not mutually exclusive but mutually supportive. When building a developer experience, a good guiding question that needs to be constantly considered is, "Are we providing an API that brings value to the consumer in their everyday work?"

Research on an API's developer experience has been scarce, which is why I researched the topic with Nazia Hasan. Based on hundreds of discussions with hundreds of API users, the following four fields share common elements central to developer experience. The list is not exhaustive but provides the foundation for building the API's developer experience.

Value creation	Easy onboarding
• Solves the problem well • Clear business models • Efficient and trust worthy	• Discoverability • Self-service • Live environment for experimentation • Well-productized SDKs/libraries • Free tier / trial
Support	**Documentation**
• Email • Phone number • Forum • Chat • API statistics and status	• Up-to-date clear documentation with code examples • Use case descriptions • Machine-readable specification • Roadmap

Table 3 A four-field model of a good developer experience

Creating Value

A good API does what it promises to do and does it well. Otherwise, the value created and experienced by an API consumer will be significantly reduced. In the case of a paid API, one should consider the price. In some cases, the price is set by experimentation and by querying potential customers. Similarly, complex business models often produce difficult-to-understand pricing that drives customers away.

In addition, an API should respond quickly and surely to each query. A slow API causes problems in the application where it is being used, thereby slowing down the entire operation. This, in turn, can ruin the user experience. If an application developer is forced to use a slow or uncertain API, he or she is forced to write additional code to his or her application, which in turn will prolong the development of the application and will increase risk factors.

Low Barriers

Nowadays, onboarding an API is expected to be self-service. Users will not be forced to ask (by email or otherwise) for IDs or API keys to access the interface.

If the API target segment cannot find the API, the search engine optimization has most likely been forgotten. In most cases, it is advisable to include the marketing department to increase the visibility of the API, as well as to carefully consider how marketing is done. Traditional marketing jargon does not work in developer relations: API consumers are most interested in solutions, not fancy phrases or slogans.

A common way to attract customers is to visit where customers are. Check out several API portals, as adding an API to them is usually free. In addition, one should consider platforms favored by different developers, such as Amazon Web Services. The latter has been applied, among others, by Finland's F-Secure.[159] One advantage of platforms and portals is that they usually handle search engine visibility. Another means for attracting users is to build a developer center. At least banks Nordea[160] and OP Financial Group[161] use this strategy.

The moment a consumer is lured into checking out product offers, a crucial window of opportunity opens – one meant to provide means for users try the API in practice, and quickly. Often, customers have asked me, "What is 'fast'?" For this purpose, I developed the 3–30–3-rule: an API consumer must understand in three seconds why the API exists (i.e., what problem it solves), try it out within 30 seconds, and within three minutes use the API from its own code. This ideal is not always reached for one reason or another. However, nowadays, some API providers seek even shorter time limits.

Setting up a paywall without offering the ability to test the interface in practice is a good way to drive potential customers to the competitor. A common strategy is to offer a limited amount of free use, during which the client can try the API, learn how to use it, and be convinced of its excellence.
In some cases, it is justifiable to provide software development kits (SDKs) to the users, the purpose of which is to facilitate the use of the API and to prepack API functionality into various development environments. Productization also applies here. Compressed as a zip file, SDK does not convince the API consumer and requires effort. Instead, productize your SDK and let the API consumers install it with packet management tools such as *npm*[162] or *pip*[163]. Consumers use package management anyway to install various software components.

Updated and Comprehensive Documentation

On Twitter, I have discussed developer experience with my network, and Antti Syrjä's comment struck a nerve: "I hate most working code examples, which don't provide any documentation. The code can never be applied to different situations 1:1." The example codes provided will not suit every situation, and thus proper documentation is essential.

One of the most important parts of the developer experience is an API's up-to-date documentation. Proper documentation includes copy-paste code examples for using API. Their purpose is to enable a quick first contact with API; that is, to create a sense of ease. In addition, the documentation should be a clear and consistent description of the API's properties.

A combination works best. The code helps one see it in practice, while documentation reveals potential. Antti Syrjä's comment speaks of a situation where the development and documentation of an API are not in sync. This, in turn, leads to a broken developer experience and frustration in experimentation and deployment. At worst, this is enough to cause an API to be discarded and for customers to pick up one offered by a competitor.

In the autumn of 2017, I interviewed four different API consumers separately for an hour regarding the introduction of an API as part of the development of the API management solution. In the interview, the users described the typical use of an API with their deployment phases, the problems encountered, and ideas for how to remove the problems. Interviews revealed typical needs, such as up-to-date documentation and code examples. In addition to these, the need to prototype freely with the API was identified. This can be done in at least two ways. HSL, presented previously, has realized the possibility of prototyping at its own level, offering a packed, data-rich API for everyone to use.

The second option is to provide a freemium plan, which makes it possible to utilize API as part of a prototype. Free usage is also an incentive that can lower the threshold to try the interface.

Occasionally, this is not possible; for example, with a partner API. In an interview, Viljami Kuosmanen, known in Finland as a long-term API developer and consumer, highlighted the need to download machine-readable API description. *Why on Earth?* From the machine-readable description, a mockup interface can be generated, with the help of ready-made tools, in its own closed development environment. A closed environment isolates application development and eliminates potential problematic situations that could otherwise be considered software errors.

When I Can't Find What I Need ...

An API is a productized service that requires support services. Although an API might offer adequate documentation, complete code examples, and clear pricing, no one can predict what issues users will encounter. Therefore, means should be provided for maintaining a dialogue with a potential customer. Minimum support can be satisfied by email and phone.

In addition to traditional channels, one should consider other channels such as forums. With those, companies have choices to make. One way is for a company to host its own forum for a developer center, for example, and hope that the users will find and use it. Another way is to use existing forums that developers already use (visiting where your customers are), such as Stack Overflow.

Elements such as analytics, which explain the situation with API – such as whether it is in operation and how it has behaved recently – offer valuable information to the users. If a company can provide this information, the user will be able to spot potential issues and make the necessary corrections. Providing information about an API's behavior also reduces direct contact with customer service, which is usually the most expensive part of customer support.

Continuous Development

Great developer experience and customer support will not last forever. The needs of users are changing, and the API needs to be versioned. The market situation is also changing, and more competition is coming.

In addition, according to lean thinking, continuous API improvement is a necessity. The API management solution brings many non-functional elements, enabling better if not excellent developer experience. An API management solution often includes API analytics for finding bottlenecks in API usage and performance.

At some point, the API also reaches the end of its life, or its version is to be retired. In the event of an API exit, developers must be informed. The sooner one can communicate to users about the exit of an API (depreciation), the more time they have to act accordingly.

Even in these situations, users appreciate information and instructions that make it easier to implement and adapt. Caring for the customer in this situation is also a mark of a company that has thought of API as a product and not just an add-on of the SaaS service. The client will not be left hanging but will be guided through each situation.

Summary

The developer experience is not just about technology or tools. A brilliant developer experience understands the needs of the users and their routes to the product and utilizes their feedback.

Free use of an API is not just a sales promotion or a free experiment but part of the developer experience, a way to offer a prospective customer a chance to explore and experiment; i.e., to learn.

A great developer experience is a selling point, while a poor developer experience ruins an opportunity to succeed in an increasingly tough API market.

The developer experience, like the API itself, is constantly evolving and requires investment.

17 PUBLISH QUICKLY, SUPPORT, MEASURE, AND LEARN

Mika Honkanen

APIs make it easy to measure things accurately. DevOps combines development and production that were previously separate. APIs are increasingly becoming part of DevOps. With a data-driven approach, an API can be developed as more customer-oriented and faster through validated learning. This chapter discusses these themes in more depth and makes the connection between interfaces, agile development, and lean startup.

Release the First Version of Your API Quickly

The first experimental version of an API should be released quickly for the potential software developers to try. It is possible to do deep research before the first API version release to understand the use cases and needs for the future product. However, it's best to move fast and validate the API usage through analytics to know what to improve or add next. Practical experience shows that it often is not possible to figure out exactly how the API will be used. By following the real-world use of an API, one gains a more solid understanding of how value is generated and what the real needs of your customers are. Often, understanding of core needs and issues is deepened following the release of an initial MVP version. It is possible that the entire idea can be transformed into a completely different direction with the help of insights learned from the MVP.

The first API release version can be thought of as a starting point for iterative learning. Once the beta or the first production version of an API is released, one will truly understand how and for what purposes the new API will be used by software developers. It allows one to determine what kind of requests are sent to the API, how developers are using it, what features from the API are used, and for what needs. One will also learn what kind of error messages are generated from the use of the API, enabling improvement of the overall user experience. With this knowledge, it is possible to improve the API documentation, code examples, and customer support. This all influences the continuous development of the API itself.

Developing an API with "lean startup" method is highly recommended[164]. The customer value dictates the features to be built, and the "build, measure, learn" (BML) cycle helps one continuously adjust and prioritize the development. A "plan, do, check, act" cycle (also known as: Deming's quality circle, PDCA) is essentially the same concept. The BML development cycle is meant for improving business activity, and the PDCA development cycle is agnostic and can be used for any process improvements.

Models support validated learning, which means that conventional hands-on work is used to validate and prove the assumptions about current and future business needs. Workflow is more practical, accurate, and faster than the earlier methods of market research or business planning. The following graphic shows the BML cycle on the left side and PDCA cycle on the right side.

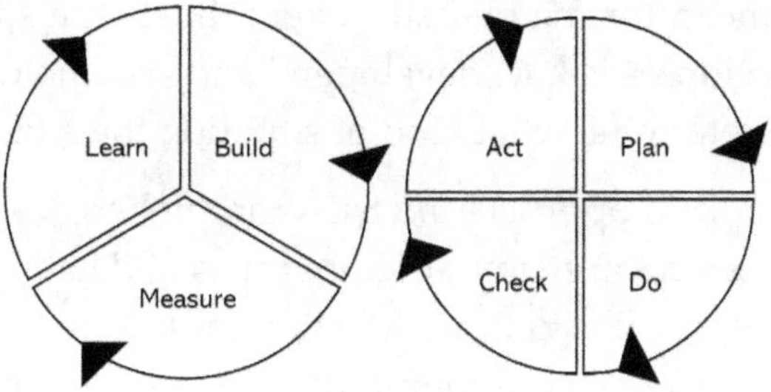

Figure 13 Even though Eric Ries is not referencing the origins of the BML model, PDCA and BML cycles are referencing similar methods. In his book, Ries mentions Deming in other contexts

The advantage of metrics from the integrated approach viewpoint is that API analytics allows the gathering of types of data not made possible via traditional web analytics. The better the BML cycle is implemented, the faster the API gradually develops to respond to customer needs.

Build an Overall View with Suitable Metrics

Measurement requires an understanding of the big picture; a technology-focused approach itself is not enough. An API's traffic can increase for many reasons, and growth might be caused either by a growing business or, alternatively, because an API is badly implemented. For example, the Finnish Patent and Registration Office (PRH) has listed on their 2015 annual report that their open-data-focused API received over 53 million requests.[165] From a positive viewpoint, that amount can sound huge, and one could assume that the API is popular. A large number of API requests can, however, be a sign of a badly designed API. Users of an API might have to do many requests to acquire the information they need, or the API itself might be technically unreliable. Tallying the amount of usage is clearly not enough, because there needs to be a clear understanding of what those details mean for the overall system. In such a situation, feedback from developers is key: developers' and stakeholders' feedback enable one to determine what kind of situation the API is facing.

It is important to approach metrics comprehensively. API usage measurement can cover many different types of details and enables a helicopter-view of the situation. Metrics are heavily condensed details about the current state and impact of an API. The overall picture is especially needed to get the business- and product-focused metrics converted to the right format. It can be difficult to measure the right things with the right approach if the understanding of the business itself is lacking. For example, we might not know whether the 53 million requests to the aforementioned PRH API are small, large, or appropriate when compared to its real demand, which is why one needs a solid understanding of how the API impacts the business needs and architecture. From that understanding, it is much more possible to build the right kinds of metrics.

Strategic measurement is done in six different fields throughout the full API lifecycle.

1. The business activity viewpoint
2. The API users' viewpoint
3. The API providers' viewpoint
4. Changes in the development and production
5. Anomalies and error amounts (related to service-level agreements and promises)
6. Information security (especially when an API is handling personal data or is publicly available)

Regardless of which viewpoint is measured, metrics change over the time as the business and operational environments develop. Metrics methods should be changed from time to time to make sure new details are uncovered, especially when measuring business-related functionality. Other sections from the metrics might stay the same for long periods of time. More important than the number of metrics used is to keep measuring relevant viewpoints. After all, you get what you measure.

Business-focused metrics are meant to improve understanding about customer needs and improve support in the building and development of a user-friendly and effective API. Metrics might vary greatly, depending on the business, the API implementation logic, and customers.

The API users' viewpoint of metrics is normally focused on API reliability, clarity, and usability. Software developers' experiences can be measured from, for example, the number of recommendations. ProgrammableWeb measures the number of people following updates to a specific APIs, the amount of comments in those APIs, how many people might be using those tools, how many articles have been written about a particular API, and what kind of support is offered for an API. A good way to gather feedback about an API is to provide a discussion platform for API development-related topics, making it possible to use that understanding for the improvement and continuous development of an API.

The following table shows some metrics from the API provider's viewpoint, which is an important part of the overall metrics. It is meant to guide development and produce valuable information for continuous development.

Topic	Target for metrics
User	Is the user a new or previous one? How fast is the API acquiring new users?

Last usage date and time	When was the most recent use?
Connection details	From where was the API contacted? Was it one's own application, a website, or something else?
Content-related requests	What file format was requested: multimedia or text? What differences exist between different content formats?
Request handling time	How fast was the request answered? Were there bottlenecks? What kinds?
Errors	What kind of error messages are users receiving, and which users?
Functionality usage	Which features of the API are being used, and which parts are not?
Needs	What new features are users wishing for?
Language (multi-language support)	What natural language (for example, Finnish) is used to make the request, and what language is used in the reply? How are language versions used?
Version control	What API version is being used? How many different versions are used, and who is using them?

Table 4 API provider viewpoint

Anomalies should measure the number and type of errors, system performance, call processing time, and delay. It is worth noting that some of the API calls can be cached so that the usage times are not displayed correctly on the server.

Information security is emerging as one key viewpoint to measure as regards APIs. The GDPR requires security to be measured more accurately in the processing of personal data. Public APIs are faced with an increasing number of security threats (e.g., denial of service attacks and experimentation with limit values).

APIs and DevOps Complement Each Other

Agile development improved the efficiency of software development with the help of independent multidisciplinary teams working in close contact with the client. Agile development also made software development more customer-oriented and faster. As a result, bottlenecks began to emerge in production.

The software industry was previously divided into two opposing groups: development and production. The goal of the development has been to produce new features and for production to reach 100% service level (no disruption or trouble). The main goal of production was stability. In practice, it is best achieved by not introducing any new features into production.

DevOps is a combination of "developers" and "operations." Its goal is to respond faster to customer needs in production and to act more like agile development. The idea is to combine previously separated functions into one seamless experience where they work together, and effectively. DevOps aims for:

1. Faster software development
2. Shorter time to market
3. Fewer failures and bugs in the code
4. Faster repair time
5. Faster fault repair

DevOps can be seen as the next evolutionary step of agile development. DevOps also extends from development to maintenance, the task of which is to produce, maintain, and support production software, which should be done as geographically close to the customer as possible. The continuous integration paradigm requires more communication with stakeholders, development automation, and more agile planning to deliver software products to the market faster than ever before.

In practice, DevOps is done using software development tools, which are increasingly being used by APIs. DevOps thinking and methods are also important for API management. API interface publications should be automated in the same manner as the application and infrastructure implementing the API. DevOps allows one to set up new development and production environments quickly and with very little effort. Many cloud platforms allow one to quite simply develop, deploy and run software in containers. For example, all of Google's software has been designed with API and containerized. When new versions are published, they are slowly released into the entire infrastructure in containers. At the same time, the functionality of the new code is quickly and automatically tested when scaled slowly to an increasing number of users. When containers work with APIs, they provide accurate information about use.

APIs can be measured precisely so that some of the measurements related to DevOps can be produced automatically. An API-based software design enables them to be partitioned into small, independent parts (microservices), making collaboration and automation easier than ever.

The following figure illustrates the DevOps structure. Although much is said about this phenomenon, it is not structured or defined in the literature. All that is done at DevOps is important for the interfaces as well.

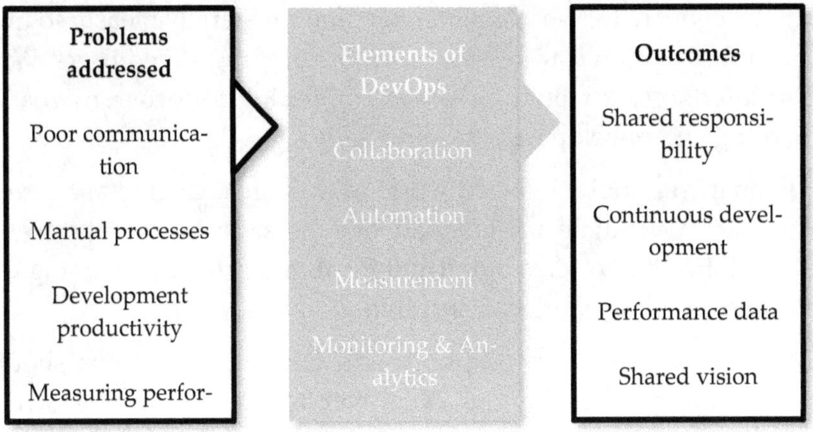

Figure 14 Everything is Measurable[166]

APIs offer a variety of support for DevOps thinking. They make it easy to collaborate, because the level of abstraction created by an API can be changed without any API consumer even noticing it. An API encapsulates the underlying software architecture and fades it out.

All data transfers through API can be accurately measured and analyzed. The information flowing through it can easily be used to find out what was done and when – within the limits of confidentiality and law, of course. This is how APIs support DevOps' goal of measuring and tracking. API can also be used to build numerous different types of automation. An API can provide a variety of data processing and testing services that can be used as tools for continuous integration and testing. For example, the quality of the data can be monitored, or the API can provide test data for the software being tested. On the other hand, by distributing the software to small, functional parts (micro-architecture), DevOps are performed more easily and quickly. Instead of developing and exporting the entire software, it can be done one part at a time; if that part does not work, the APIs can be upgraded and returned to the previous version. State-level open data sharing interfaces have generally measured traffic volumes and, in some cases, the number of registered users. With open interfaces, it would be worth continuing to focus on what is emerging and developing regarding APIs.

In an increasingly digitized world, things are changing at an ever-faster pace. Only agile and innovative organizations have a future, as they will be able to seize opportunities that can lead to ongoing development of new, market-disruptive products.

Instead of making assumptions and taking guesses, one should take advantage of continuous experimentation and learning, which allows one to change direction on the fly. If the original idea is not sensible, a pivot is worth considering – that is, changing direction. Reasons to pivot may be that the customer's problem is misunderstood, or the MVP indicates that the idea is not commercially viable.

Summary

The first version of the API should be made available to developers quickly. Measuring and evaluating feedback is crucial.

Use analytics to ensure that development is guided correctly (validated learning).

An API can measure usage of the system more accurately than web analytics.

DevOps brings agility to software production. Its goal is to improve communication, automate operations, develop measurement and monitoring, and improve collaboration with software development.

API management and DevOps have largely the same goals: it is advisable to automate the API release and measure the API usage, as well as the application layer that implements it.

API output enhances both DevOps and agile software development.

SECTION IV: MANAGING APIS

18 EXPOSED INTERFACES

Marjukka Niinioja

Do I need API management and separate API management tools? Do we know what interfaces we have, and who will use and develop them? Are inboxes packed with API documentation, and do they ever match implementation? In this chapter, we seek answers to these questions.

API management remained a "nonproblem" for a long time. In small businesses, developers were responsible for APIs, and they often only trusted their own code. Business models, and the transformation of them into networked or platformed, were not a hot topic in most companies; the APIs were either part of a larger system or a set of early microservices. Usually, only one cloud was used for a few internally developed applications, so the need for API management was not well understood. Dozens of commercial closed or open source API management products with different features existed on the market. Some had limited support for DevOps, and most of them were geared toward monetization of APIs. API management was an island located between traditional integrations, microservices, and proxy servers, providing very little support for the large-scale deployment of cloud services and distributed solutions. The utmost feeling of IT personnel in companies was confusion. The related meetings went roughly like this:

– *"We need API management."*

– "Does it mean that we have a single point through which all services go, and if it fails, everything stands still?"

– "Why do we need API management for APIs used by only one application?"

We are now at the stage in Finland (not dissimilar to the situation in other countries) where many large companies and public sectors are introducing an API management solution, at least for internal and partner APIs. Businesses have a growing understanding of the need to renew their business models and adapt their API strategies to their business strategies.

The introduction of API management, either an API management technology or product, is not just a technical matter. API management also includes an API or developer portal, as well as an API catalog or an "API store" from which API users can access APIs, either independently or by requesting permissions. Most importantly, through the developer portal, the organization sees what interfaces it owns: what it has developed, bought or subscribed. The developers can also see the available APIs and will be able to familiarize themselves with the API's documentation and then test it. At the same time, they can choose the level of service that suits their needs and even their budgets (e.g., 100 requests per day). The developer portal and other resources available to developers are an important part of the developer experience discussed in chapter 16.

One can communicate, support, and advertise interfaces or even the entire organization through the developer portal or, more broadly, the developer center. If a company has a website targeted toward developers introducing its APIs or SDKs (typically something like developers.yourcompany.com, dev.yourcompany.com or api.yourcompany.com), it will garner significant credibility and visibility in terms of employer brand or innovative and open solution provider. From a recruitment perspective, the developer portal helps the company become, for example, modern and developer-oriented. It also enhances the company's image as an open and innovative actor and encourages partnership.

However, not all APIs need to be external and not all need to be published on the portal for all user groups. Because it is a service that requires search engine optimization for internal or external search engines, content production, and visualization, it should be treated as one site among others. Of course, the developer portal should receive most of its content automatically via the API publishing process and Open API descriptions, but it is only part of the content. Also consider who lends the rights to use an API, how to make decisions, and who really clicks the button.

In many countries with a long tradition of productization and product management, such as the UK and the US, an API's overall responsibility lies with API product managers, who oversee commercialization and productization, even if it is only for internal use. They meet with the communication, marketing, and sales departments to discuss how APIs should be brought into the company's offering and how their interests should be communicated to decision-makers and experts. They also take care of the development plan and ensure that the business and customer needs are considered. They collaborate daily with product development teams.

Confusion persists, however – at least in many Finnish companies but also elsewhere – on roles and responsibilities. Most companies employ business-responsible developers of digital services, software developers, and integration experts. All these experts think either that they are in charge of the company APIs and API management or that someone else should be. An ideal scenario would feature more companies that really embrace APIs as a digital business solution and part of the company's offering itself. An API is not integration, and API management is not an integration platform.

At the time of this writing, Finland is just waking up to the need for API management solutions. In the meantime, API management has taken a huge leap into the larger cloud platform ecosystem. Business and public sector ecosystems are emerging. Public sector programs for platform and API-based technologies, such as artificial intelligence, block chains, and the IoT, have been launched. Managed ecosystems require API management.

Since early 2017, the needs for companies to choose an API management solution has been on the rise, usually as part of the ongoing integration of environmental renewal. Many organizations looked at API management products and were confused about the options available from different technology vendors. The choice was difficult, because it was no longer purely a matter of technology but of what technology ecosystem the company wanted to belong to or what business strategy it was pursuing.

Towards the end of 2017, there arose the hope that future business models and ecosystems would be considered when making API management decisions. It may not be worthwhile to invest in the appearance of a developer portal, for example, if within the next five years the user base will only be internal (if, say, the company does not start networking even though its competitors are). Instead, it is worth investing in a solution that supports the company's business or IT strategy, like multi-cloud environments or monetizing API usage, depending on the needs. It is worth examining API management as a business application and as part of a cloud strategy.

Compared to previous years, discussions about API management solutions are now more straightforward:

– "You want API management? Ok, but what is your business strategy?"

– "What else are you going to do in the cloud? Do you have API applications like AI, bots, blockchain, or IoT?"

– "What is your company's core competence, and what is the customer journey you envision and the ecosystem you want to join?"

– "What is your most important service, knowledge, digital, or human or physical resource? Who do you think brings value to customer paths or the ecosystem you are part of (i.e., what interfaces should your company offer)?"

– "How can others make money and innovate with your APIs?"

Can an API Exist Without API Management?

Several API management solutions based on a proxy server or a mandatory HTTP gateway solution as part of a cloud service are available. As a garnish, they usually contain a touch of a tailor-made or separate service for access control, identification, and custom-tuned analytics. With these, no developer portal has been built, but documentation has generally been maintained manually or by generating scripts with HTML pages from API specifications.

For some purposes, this is enough. For example, with one SaaS ERP application project I was involved in, the distribution of API keys was done directly inside the application, and it was a perfectly adequate solution. If we had wanted to monetize our APIs and charge for them separately, we would have implemented the functionality using, for example, a payment transfer API and some SaaS service. The starting point for the decisions was that human labor was inexpensive and did not require separate decisions, while the price tags (in year

2014) for API management solutions were a bit steep for a small-scale operation.

Without full API management, it would have been impossible to handle even an operation of that size. Traffic had to be restricted and data processing regulated. At the same time, the system contained turnover and cost information for large Finnish and international companies, not to mention employee and customer information. Implementing API analytics was perhaps the most painful step after identity management and authentication. Available analytics tools were meant to be used only for web-based server-side traffic. The main tool was a low-cost software program, which could not easily be used to share reports even within the company, let alone API users themselves. Approximately 20 separate APIs were used, and their documentation was based on a RAML description, a very new, standardized description method for which tools for generating documentation were found – and which at the time was the only one available.

This solution worked well, because the API was built for a relatively monolithic system based on our own product development. The API could be produced and managed with the system's own functions quite easily, and it was possible to provide access to it using one web address and one physical location, without any proxy services.

Decentralized API Management in a Large Enterprise

After six months as Kesko API Development Manager, I wrote of my experiences:

We have 100+ APIs in use or in progress and a huge number of teams. Most teams do not have any experience with API management solutions, and they do not even want to know about them. So, we needed something especially for development processes and a continuous deployment of software release (CI – continuous integration and CD – continuous deployment) processes. Thus, we were able to keep API interfaces at the same level as the implementation layer. APIs work on different platforms (Heroku, AWS, On-premise, etc.) and are written in different languages (mostly Node.js and Java). Most APIs run in the cloud, and almost all use internal network services as part of their implementation.

API management and integration tools are needed for routing secure data between public and private clouds and for the local area network. API management increases security and usability. It displays internal or external addresses of the API for API users, depending on which area of the network the users use the API. All APIs are displayed as kesko.fi addresses, regardless of their original addresses, like s3-website-us-west-2.amazonaws.com.

At the time of writing those notes (February 2017), only part of the interfaces passed through API management. The release of previously deployed interfaces via API management would have required changes to both the API and its user interface. Not all APIs were described using the Open API specification required by our API management product. The developer portal was being introduced, and the biggest challenges were to decide who in the organization should be responsible for maintaining, developing, and managing it. API management as a technical solution was given to the integration team, because it was thought to be an integration solution. API development belonged to those responsible for digital services. The developer portal, on the other hand, was more of a website, and its ownership was initially uncertain. The biggest challenges were to find the right people, establish API publishing processes in different teams, and create API development methods and descriptions suitable for the API management product.

As said earlier, a good API developer is naturally lazy and proficient in doing so. He or she doesn't want to know anything about API management – at least not about technology – because from their point of view, their API works perfectly without it, too. However, large organizations are forced to have apply a management process and a technical solution to support it. No one would otherwise know which APIs are already available or who uses them. A good compromise must be found for legal reasons, too, especially when APIs are located in multiple environments and are developed by many teams.

So, one should make sure that the API management product or solution can automate all API lifecycle measures. Automation can be done using the tools provided by the API management solution, such as the command line interface (CLI), API, or plugin for the software used by the development team to automate software testing and deployments (e.g., Jenkins, Travis CI, etc.). The developer does not want to do anything other than write "commit" when committing code to the version control. He or she hopes that all tests, publications, and installations in the runtime environment will automatically take place in the publishing process, and that some trendy discussion environment (like Slack or Teams) integrated into the process will alert him or her if something goes wrong.

In most API management products, in addition to the API configuration (usually Open API), an API product specification or other configuration file is required. It describes an API's "product features," i.e., what alternative levels (such as usage) are available to API users. The file also defines monetization and service levels for the API, as well as a possible acceptance workflow to allow developers to take the API into use. The definition or configuration information also usually describe the API authentication method and the publishing environment in the API management. Then, certain APIs can be published only on the internal network. Depending on the networking solutions, the applications running inside the internal network can use them on internal network addresses not accessible to external users. Other security features can also be associated with API management solutions; for example, features that can verify authentication when using the token that comes with the API call from a trusted source and assess whether it is still valid.

Exceptions and Other Oddities

With API management solutions, one might feel like Shakespeare's Hamlet, asking, "To manage or not to manage, that is the question." For example, if you create a composite service – that is, a microservice that in turn calls other interfaces – should these calls be routed through the API management? In most cases, the answer lies in the actual location of the API. How do you isolate the problem if one of the APIs does not respond? If APIs are offered in the same cloud and close together, the problem may not be a major one. If the APIs under the composite service are also directly used by other services, it may be wise to manage these requests via API management. At least if the API gateway component of the API management solution is installed in the same environment as the services, any possible delays in communication will be minimized.

Other problems lie in those where the API is only used by one user or application; for example, if a mobile application stores information about the user in the application's user settings. Do these APIs also need to be placed under API management? Can they even be called APIs in the first place? In most cases, this type of an interface is used by one application, and the data content is not particularly sensitive, so API management may not be required. The only problem is that from the point of view of the coder, more similar needs immediately surface. These new needs may contain sensitive information or may be useful for other services. In this case, there are grounds for publishing the API via API management, but how does one distinguish between scenarios? "I would recommend using API management as a de facto solution; only if the API management solution is proven to be detrimental should a decision be made case-by-case."

Sometimes, there arises a need for something other than API. The API can be provided, for example, with the help of GraphQL, which is sort of like database queries made to interfaces. In general, GraphQL and other similar solutions use a different URI design than the REST APIs and operate in different ways from the point of view of user authentication and management[167]. It should also be noted that GraphQL often uses one or more REST APIs to retrieve data. GraphQL endpoints can't usually be managed with API management tools intended for REST APIs, but that does not mean they don't need to be managed at all, the tools are just different and there are some different design points. We discussed the GraphQL vs. REST API management in an APIOps Helsinki meetup in August 2018, at that time the market saw only Apollo and AWS providing any technical solutions and the topic is still quite fresh as you can see from the blog post and collected references, I wrote from our session[168].

Sometimes, a traditional REST API is not the right solution. It is better to do a "push" by the API provider to the API consumer when something changes in the provider's system, rather than a "polling" solution where the API consumer constantly checks for new information on the provider's end. The "push" paradigm is used, for example, in IoT solutions where huge amounts of sensor data are received.

The IoT, the Internet of Things, sets its own requirements for API management, because each device has its own API and devices, which means the number of APIs is huge. IoT devices also use lighter protocols, such as MQTT instead of HTTP. In his research, Aziz[169] provides perspectives on and insight into why API management in the IoT world is more challenging. To solve this challenge, separate IoT platforms have been included in many cloud services.

Summary

API management is still young, and technology and offerings from providers have only developed in recent years.

The need for API management and technology depends on both business needs and architecture.

The developer center is a key part of an API's developer experience and communication.

API publishing often takes place automatically when the API is released to API management.

It is advisable to describe the APIs with Open API (or other means supported by that API management) so that the API documentation is automatically generated to the portal.

It is advisable to place the API management's runtime component, the API gateway, as close to the API as possible. Or, at least, it is worth protecting the traffic between API management and the API backend.

Internal APIs also require API management.

Not all APIs or API-enabled technologies are suitable for being managed with all API management products, and there are also dedicated platforms for IoT interfaces.

19 DISTRIBUTE AND MANAGE

Marjukka Niinioja

This chapter discusses implementation under the API, i.e. the interface. Does the API always need to do be implemented with microservices? Does the microservice always have to provide an API? What about the old systems – how are they "APIfied"?

Does an API always need microservices?

An API should be programming-language-agnostic, meaning it shouldn't favor or depend on any particular language. The API consumer should not see nor need to care in which programming language or system the application logic behind it has been implemented or in which environment the application layer is run. It can often even be considered a security risk, but at the very least it is unnecessary information for the API user.

Previously, very different solutions were considered as APIs, such as web services using SOAP protocol based on SOA architecture and various services provided over the HTTP protocol.

Today, API, especially REST API, refers to an architectural and design style. It is particularly suitable for use over the internet and can be used with several different communication protocols. "REST" only refers to how the interface is designed (as resources). It works seamlessly, utilizing HTTP methods[170] and hypertext. SOA-style APIs use WSDL description and XML presentation. The REST API can use several different specification standards, the most common now being Open API. The format and content type of the request can be anything, even sound, image, or PDF files. In most cases, however, JSON is used because it is well suited for modern user interface technologies and is lighter than XML.

Distributed architecture, and because of that microservices, can be a justified option for API development, especially if the digital platform and services are developed at the same time. However, the solution requires that micro and other services be managed at some level. Why? To know what services an organization owns, who uses and maintains them, in what environment they are located, what data they handle, and how secure they are. If services provide APIs for other services to use and these APIs are published via API management, the services become easier to manage.

Decentralized management, for which microservices were essentially invented, provides certain opportunities for architectural design. In their research[171], Di Fransesco (2017) and others list the benefits, stating that as a microservice, services are independent, can be implemented with appropriate technologies, and gradually renew the architecture. Microservices are particularly well-suited to the cloud, because they can utilize the cloud's flexibility and fast service provisioning capability. Running them in cloud also poses challenges: network latency and unreliability, fault tolerance, data consistency, and transaction management, as well as the number of communication layers and load balancing.

Peck[172] lends a centralized perspective in his blog about what is particularly ideal in microservices: developers can choose the technology that is right for the purpose and that is particularly well known by the team for each service. Architectural and software development principles can be kept at a general level, and each team manages their own environment and development tools.

This means that services should not depend on one another at code-level, except via the API. It is often tempting within the same team to use one's own microservices directly, for example, with JavaScript or programming language API. This should be the exception, as needs may arise to replace the microservice, for example, with an API provided by another party. Or, possibly, the service needs to be moved to a different physical location. In this case, it is not very safe and sensible to call another component at the code level.

The limits of the freedom to choose technology must be determined. In large organizations, technology choices are limited to ensure expertise and continuity. Wingelhofer and Aistleitner (2017) list examples of such companies: Spotify, Soundcloud, and PegahTech Co., and note that the reasons for the restrictions are not clear and require further research, since if the selection proves to be incorrect, the microservices are small and easy to change within a few weeks.[173]

The best solution is not always to do what is most convenient now for the user interface or backend coder. One must find out what the purpose of the service is and how it should be scaled and distributed, for example. Is the code intended to be used by only a handful of users? Is the application running in a single server? Is logic available for just one interface? What will happen in a few months? Typically, a well-working service is immediately expanded to new user segments, which requires scaling the architecture and in turn, more distributed design.

Microservice models are available for different uses. Take, for example, a new customer registration. It could happen like this:

1. First, one checks to see if a customer can be found in the register by email. If not, more information if requested.

2. One checks the given email address by sending an email with a link for confirmation.

3. Only when the link is clicked can one make sure that the customer is registered.

However, there may be cases where the workflow is slightly different; for example, in some services or for some customer groups, it is more important to check the phone number instead of email. In that situation, the first thing to do is case A, then B, and, depending on the case, either C or D.

Is it that the user interface needs to be able to call the APIs in the correct order? Suppose that four microservices are required to implement functionality, all of which already provide APIs. Wouldn't the user interface just call them?

What if the user interface gets implemented sloppily and does not call the email service via API and thus doesn't ask for a confirmation email?

It is important for business and legal purposes to know that the user is a particular, identified human. Can this issue be left to the user interface? The user interface can be reliable in itself, be it made with one's own or purchased technology, but still, one can forget or accidentally change the application controls, or the code can become disarrayed. In that case, there is a risk that one step will be missed in the checks. What if, for example, a user's network was temporarily disconnected mid-process? Can the user continue with the process, or should someone manually update the database?

What about multichannel and multiple user interfaces? First, one implements a web application running on a web browser and then, as an afterthought, a mobile application. In some cases, the user interface is a cash register or a refrigerator. They use the same process, so there are two options:

1. Each implementer must be sure to understand how the process goes and consider any changes over the lifecycle.

2. Business logic and workflow control should be built into the service providing the API, even if it would have to use other (micro) services as part of its implementation.

The microservice architecture may not conflict with the benefits of large systems. It brings many benefits, according to Cuestan et al. (2018):[174]

- Services can be developed in small parts.
- Services can be developed around business capabilities.
- Development can be organized by product and not be project-specific, thus ensuring continuity and expertise.
- The "smart endpoints and dumb pipes" principle encourages the use of simple protocols such as HTTP/S and for one to keep up with data transmission and processing close to the basic principles of the web.
- The above-mentioned principles contribute to the independence of services and facilitate geographical decentralization and the independence of the technology. Changes implemented may also cause a change to a single function, not the entire system.

Source of Eternal Youth

There are cases where a large (traditional) monolithic system needs to be concealed with an API so other systems can integrate with the API and not the monolith directly. This "face lift" may be done in order to get rid of the monolith at some point. How should we "APIfy" that?

Sometimes, one sees major product upgrades of self-developed software platforms. The need originating from the business-side decision-makers is to cover traditional business applications with a modern API that supports digital services.

I especially recall a particularly complicated case of APIfying an in-house legacy system. We were wondering how to start modifying the system to meet modern requirements. In the original solution, all parts of the user interface implemented some of the business logic. The team wondered if anything could be done when the old code and the system were holding us back. Were we part of the technical "backwater"?

It is not entirely clear that microservices are the only option. Many big organizations have not yet dared to jump on board: as an architectural model, it only started to become popular in 2014.[175] If a company has previously built its own software product, rebuilding it using microservices is hardly sensible just because it is trendy. However, its decentralization may be justified. In large companies, APIs have often been seen as merely a form of integration, and thinking has been that the transformation capabilities of integration platforms can be used to adequately manage all types of services.

Traditional systems are often not service-oriented. However, they possess a lot of functionality that could be provided as a service. It is essential to be able to reuse the functionality as easily as possible to rebuild such a system. The rebuilding process consists of three stages:[176]

- Thorough exploration of system functions to find service candidates
- Packaging of functionalities into services
- Modification of system implementation to provide services

Different traditional system implementation techniques offer varying degrees of ease in providing functional services; for example, using the REST API architecture principles. Often, the goal is to use the API layer to slowly replace the entire previous system. Users would not notice anything because user interfaces and integrations have been implemented with API.

This is an admirable goal, but it requires exceptional and accurate control of the implementers in order for the API to become truly fit for the purpose. The API must not reveal any old system's data models, error messages, or functional "peculiarities." It must be implemented so that the application logic and the interface-producing layer are sufficiently differentiated from the system itself. This is often the hardest part, because the implementation of the API is hurried or has other constraints. It is simply easier to implement the API to "look right" and have it still tied to the old system.

The rebuilding project must then be prepared to make an API exactly like or at least sufficiently similar to the old one. However, one should consider change is inevitable. The fact that the previous system is attached to its users with an API and database queries or contains a messy code base will underscore the need to migrate.

Summary

Microservices should often provide APIs.

An API can be implemented with both microservices and a monolith.

In a distributed architecture, often based on microservices, the importance of API management is growing. It is important to be able to transfer and scale-up services without interfering with user behavior or revealing where services are located and how they are implemented.

In decentralized management, teams can choose the most appropriate technologies for each solution, but the choice of technology is often limited in the name of learning, continuity, and manageability.

20 IDENTITY CRISIS

Marjukka Niinioja

This final chapter explores the challenges facing API users and their identity management, authentication, and access management. In addition, this chapter discusses solutions for situations where the user has multiple identities, depending on the uses or where APIs require different levels of access management solutions. For example, should your API user be an adult citizen of Finland or a customer's contact person related to a specific agreement?

Right Access Control Matters

Previously, the API was seen solely as a means of communication between systems (and especially server software). The servers and their trusted software were "safe." Even the communication between them went through the same network or a secure connection. The data was read from one database through part of an application and written into another database. The data change was made by the "System User," "Administrator," or some other master user, and everything was fine.

With mobile services, single-page applications, and the IoT, API usage and user management experienced a revolution of sorts. It was no longer possible to use the API with the tokens given to the application, because the communications were running on the public internet or the entity calling the API was not reliable. The software was no longer located on a secure server but on a client device such as a mobile phone, a user's computer, or a microchip installed on a test tube (the kind they use in a laboratory). In other words, the API and its keys were easy to decode or detect by viewing network traffic in the web browser. The API security could be breached by almost any user with slightly-above-average technical skills.

Solutions were needed that identified both the software (sometimes also the device) and the person currently using the software. The best solution developed so far is OpenID Connect.[177]

Most social media services use OpenID Connect-based authentication – also for an API. Most of them use their own APIs. Each service offers its own solutions for many user devices. This technological aspect has contributed to the fact that the use of social media user accounts and information is highly common.

For example, a meeting and event space reservation API provided by the City of Helsinki identifies users using YLE (the public broadcasting service in Finland), Facebook, Google, and Twitter IDs. This is important because OpenID Connect and the basic user information that accompany it help limit functionality to only the user. Although it is not a state secret if you have booked a meeting room for the evening, your booking should not, however, be editable by others, and you may simply not want others to see it. Identifying API users via social media is indeed useful for APIs that require personal identification but do not require security, which is the case with e-government. There is no need in knowing which Matti of many you are, as long as your email address and, accordingly, your Google ID is matti.mottonen123@gmail.com.

Solutions for strong API identification also exist. The public sector in Finland generally uses the Suomi.fi (Suomi=Finland) service, which identifies users against the population information system with electronic bank credentials or an electronic identity card. This makes it possible to ascertain whether the user is the actual, and registered, person he or she claims to be. It is also possible to determine the age of the API user. This need will be met both in the handling of public sector forms and applications and, for example, in the APIs of a company selling alcohol (in Finland, the state has a monopoly on alcohol, and the age limit is 18).

Suomi.fi originally used only Security Markup Language (SAML) authentication. SAML[178] causes almost physical pain for a developer belonging to the REST generation.

Authenticating a REST API with SAML, which needs a separate security token service is as useful as recharging a cell phone battery by burning coal. Fortunately, thanks to the EU directive on open banking, the Suomi.fi service is also available as an OpenID Connect solution[179], which is considerably more suitable for safe and modern APIs. It also includes extensions for OpenID Connect to provide private identification information. OpenID Connect even offers slightly faster response times than SAML, which is important when the usage rates are high.

An OpenID Connect-compatible authentication service can be connected with API management. The connection, used for validating the authentication information, can be done either in real time or "offline" so the public key of the authentication service is stored in the API management. It can open the "token" that an API-enabled application deposits in an API call to the authorization header, just like the address on an envelope. In that case, however, the token, i.e., the "address," is encrypted. API management can ensure that API calls are signed with a trusted authentication service key and that the token is still valid. If everything is correct, the API management will allow the call to go through to the application providing the API.

A token can contain various "claims," i.e., identifiers, and personal information concerning the user: an email address, a customer number, or a business ID. It is essential that the authentication service has written these claims to the token when the user is identified. The application using the API cannot, therefore, change the claims. The application layer that implements the API may, for example, limit the customer data to be returned to the particular customer whose number has come with the token.

Is your identity based on email?

Authentication is based on user identity. It sounds simple: I am me, you are you, and we are separate individuals. Often, in services that are not electronic, people are identified by their email address, sometimes by phone number. Email addresses are always unique. However, one person may have several email addresses. One can be a work address, one personal, and some of us have several of both. The same person can sometimes use the same email address when acting as a member of the board of an association and as a member of a local community applying for a spot for their child in daycare. These identities must not be combined unintentionally.

A person must be able to choose the relationship for which he or she will register the email address for different purposes. In some cases, the service must limit the allowed options. For example, the service may require that the email address belongs to a trusted domain.

Often, the email address may be the only mandatory information for a user and the one guaranteed to be in the same format in different systems. Therefore, in the API world, it is quite common that the email address from the authentication service is used for access control, as if it were a user role. However, it is also necessary to require additional checks per API – for example, the registration number of the association and the email address of the person – before the API agrees to seek information about the person's signatory rights for that association.

To keep things interesting, we must also keep in mind those services and APIs that contain both internal and external users. Consider an example of a resident applying for a building permit, in which an official of the municipality deals with the application. A person living in a municipality must identify herself using the population register, and the officer in charge of building permits must do so against the municipal user directory. Both must have access to the same "building permit API" to retrieve information about either their own building permit applications (the resident) or applications from property owners (the official).

In both cases, API management should be able to verify that the authentication request came from a trusted entity, even if the authentication services for residents and officials are separate and both groups of users are using the same API. The "Building Permit API" should be able to return only the data of the persons or properties in question, based on the identifiers in the token that comes with the API call. Some parts of the information may be public and required to be returned by the API, regardless of who is making the call. The alternative is to design either an API where the authentication is much more lightweight but does not contain any confidential information or to keep the stronger authentication and use the same API.

Companies, too, have requirements to support different user groups in the same APIs or at least in the same API management. In the retail refund process, when the consumer returns a product, the seller or clerk processes the refund and pays the customer either the value of the product in cash, credit or as an alternative product. In e-commerce, this process requires the support of an API, and part of the process can still take place "offline." The same refund transaction is handled by at least a consumer and store employee, possibly a store manager and the accounting department. Visibility and access are typically restricted for each role.

Creating a new refund transaction (POST /refunds) can usually only be allowed for the customer, but some operations should also be allowed for the seller, such as accepting the refund or changing the status to "handled." The customer can only earn a refund for products purchased. Although the seller authenticates himself to use the

API, he must also be able to modify customer information data, if needed, such as the loyalty card number. On the other hand, the seller is the only one who can mark the purchase to be refunded as received and processed, so the POST /refunds/ {id} API call may only be allowed to be used by the store employees and provided as a separate API.

Another challenge is to restrict the API using partners' contract-based access to partnership-related data. For example, a toilet paper manufacturer is interested in the sales volume of its products in a particular retail chain. The manufacturer is also interested in analytics, such as ones that explain which products sell the most in certain areas, on what days, and to which customer segments. However, the toilet paper manufacturer is usually only allowed to view its own sales statistics and possibly the overview of the market share as compared to other manufacturers. The authentication service must, therefore, fetch a contract number or other identifier for the API to be able to limit the information it serves to the contract parties.

The essential elements in these cases is not to trust the API consumer calling the API to give the correct identifiers. One should also avoid "hardcoding" the contract identifiers with the API keys provided by the API management. It significantly slows down the deployment process of new API users if you always require changes to the code.

Naik and Jenkins (2017) have compared why OpenID Connect is better than SAML or OAuth2 for authenticating REST APIs and determined:[180]

- The latest standard (2014) supports federated identity management (FIdM) and single-sign-on login for users
- It utilizes of JSON and JWT standards (JSON Web Token)
- The token contains identity but no credentials
- HTTP, REST architecture, and JSON format are employed

- It requests permission from the user before sharing user information
- It supports decentralized and combined claims
- It supports the revoking of permissions but also authentication with the use of an encrypted and signed ID token without requiring access to the authentication service
- Signature is done with JSON Web Signature (JWS) and HMAC SHA-256
- Encryption is done with JSON Web Encryption (JWE) with 2048-bit key (more secure than SAML or OAuth2)
- It's suitable for both browser and mobile applications (including IoT) and to secure API management and microservice traffic if located on different networks
- It's better suited for both business and consumer use than SAML
- It's a lightweight standard, especially compared to SAML
- It's an open standard for platform and supplier-independent support, but it also supports dynamic registration, which was omitted from OAuth 2.0
- It scales perfectly as standard implementation, unlike SAML and even OAuth 2.0
- Matching GSMA Mobile Connect standard with OpenID Connect is ongoing at http://openid.net/wg/mobile/

Summary

Most client applications and devices used on the internet are unsafe. Thus, authentication solutions that recognize both the application and the user, often even the device, are needed.

One API may have multiple user groups. All user groups must be identified and authenticated using the relevant user management for each group, and the authentication information must be safely passed through API management to the API.

One user may have multiple identities. At times, strong identification is required. A more lightweight solution is sometimes good enough, often one based on accounts used for social media or common cloud services.

The user's identity is often based on an email address, and the user may need to use a different identity or at least a different email address for services from the same provider.

Authentication should be done in a method suitable for the API's implementation technique. Usually, the REST API should use OpenID Connect-based authentication for internet and mobile.

EPILOGUE

While reading the book, you, the reader may have wondered why we have not defined the main concept, the API economy. Before we started the book project, we authors were painfully conscious of the vagueness of the term. Then, while writing the book, we became certain that the term was still relatively new and its future uncertain.

There is hardly any mention of the API economy in research literature. During the writing process, we discussed how to define the term. The conversations were ongoing daily, and many times continued well into the night. At some point, Jarkko stated, "We define the platform economy, the ecosystem, and API, but if we do not define the API economy. We will look foolish, because it is the main concept of the book."

Finally, when the chapters were starting to take shape, we came to the conclusion that because the other chapters of the book discuss the API economy through practical examples, the definition of the API economy should be placed at the *end* of the book. While reading the previous chapters, you have encountered dozens of examples and perspectives on the API economy, and we now define the API economy as follows:

In the API Economy, a company utilizes resources efficiently and quickly to create added value for customers. These resources can be, for example, data or a function provided by other organizations.

The building blocks consist of one's own APIs and open APIs provided by other organizations (free or commercial) as well as those offered by developer communities. These enable more efficient adaptability for unpredictable and quickly changing customer needs.

Defining characteristics of the API Economy are competition for popularity among application developers and consideration of them as primary customers. In brief, services are offered as B2D, businesses-to-developer.

The structure of the book remained as planned during the writing process. In the first part, we investigated how business models and interfaces relate to each other through examples related to various companies, organizations, and industries. In particular, we focused on the business models, platforms, and APIs that enable the API economy and how the interfaces based on customer needs and the orchestration of interfaces provided by external parties create new business. We used Finnish companies and communities as examples and compared them to internationally renowned counterparts.

In the second part, we explored the diverse nature of the API. Interfaces are developed for many purposes: for internal use to save costs, time, and other resources; for partners to expand their own businesses; for customers to use as a building block for new services; or a completely public model for bringing about innovations. Developer communities are customers like any others, and they are an important part of a corporate, affiliate, and employee brand. Interfaces developed jointly with the developer community will always be better than those created in an organizational vacuum. In addition, new end-user innovations and more coherent customer experience also create more loyal, satisfied, profitable, and scalable customer relationships.

In the third part, we looked at API management and development as a process. We immersed ourselves in the transformation that APIs undergo in a company's internal operations and organization models. We recognized the challenge of getting business developers, marketers, lawyers, and IT architects, as well as security, product, and integration experts (from software developers), to work via common methods and with common language. A company risks losing business to competitors due to slow and poor-quality API development, as well as unsafe and unprotected interfaces that require a lot of manual work to manage, maintain, and market.

Part four explored the specific issues of the API economy caused by industry-specific legislation, organizational and operations models, and personal data processing requirements. Some of the items discussed were when to use API management and how it affects customer experience, user volumes, and security requirements. How should outdated systems and processes be transported to API era? What if an API contains sensitive information protected by legislation? What if an API is a way to expand the business abroad, or if users reside in market areas where specific requirements are set – for example, for use of personal data?

Writing this book took an incredible effort from us, especially when we had only four months to do the Finnish version and a few months more to translate and edit the English edition. All authors have families and demanding jobs. Thus, a big thank-you to our employers, colleagues, friends, and above all our families for making this possible. Thank you very much, members of our Finnish Facebook group, those who participated in the exchange of thoughts under the hashtags #APItalous101 and #APIeconomy101 on Twitter, and those with whom we have had excellent discussions during the writing of the book. Without you and your questions and your encouragement and your ideas, we would not have survived the writing process and the book would not have become so comprehensive.

For the English edition, we hesitated whether to pursue it or not, but the enthusiastic feedback for the Finnish version and the encouragement and interest of our international network made us go the extra mile. Translating a book from Finnish is not an easy task: the vocabulary, grammar, and idioms are so vastly different. To author an edition that would make sense for an international audience and non-Finnish-speaking audience in Finland felt even more challenging. We hope we preserved some interesting local flavor while still helping readers outside Finland with their particular challenges.

We appreciate your thoughts and feedback. You can contact us on social media or send feedback to the email address provided on the copyright page of the book. We wish all you of API enthusiasts a grand adventure and great success with the API economy!

GLOSSARY

We included an English-Finnish glossary in the book, because many API-related terms are commonly used in English amid Finnish text or discussion, and because we wanted you to appreciate the task in translating the book, due to such differences in the language.

Added Value *(Lisäarvo)*

The value that the customer experiences and benefits from using a product or service.

API *(API, ohjelmointirajapinta, rajapinta)*

Application programming interface that allows different applications to share information, functionality, and resources with others. The API can be a REST API, i.e., it can be used on the internet regardless of the programming language, or it can be the interface of a programming language or library.

API Catalog *(API-katalogi)*

A site where API providers can enter information about their interfaces to gain visibility and customers. May contain also API management functionality.

API Consumer *(API-hyödyntäjä)*

The application developer using interfaces.

API Developer *(API-kehittäjä)*

An application developer who develops or consumes interfaces.

API Development *(API-kehitys)*

A type of software development that specializes in APIs and uses interface-friendly methods and tools to complement more general software development methods and tools. Similar to *user interface development.*

API Gateway *(API Gateway)*

An API management service component through which API calls from the calling system to the API-implementing system are routed. The API gateway implements the rules defined in the API management solution to restrict, identify, and control traffic.

API Management *(API-hallinta)*

Both the processes in which interfaces are developed, maintained, and shared and the API management tools.

API Management Platform *(API-hallintatyökalu)*

A platform that often includes features for publishing, limiting, documenting, versioning, and enabling interfaces. May include functions for managing users, policies, pricing, visibility, etc., as well as a developer portal and API gateway.

API Marketplace *(API-markkinapaikka)*

A platform for API sales; a kind of online store for APIs.

API Provider *(API-tarjoaja)*

An interface provider, usually an organization but can also be an individual.

API Style Guide *(API-tyyliohje)*

A guide that controls the development of APIs by creating the conditions to maintain interfaces and lifecycles; a means for standardizing API design, development, and style.

Artificial Intelligence (AI) (Tekoäly)

The ability of a computer or other machine to perform intelligent activities, normally associated with humans. . Examples include machine vision, speech recognition, and production. Artificial intelligence requires a lot of data, computing power, and algorithms. Most applied artificial intelligence and machine learning solutions are available via API interfaces.

Boundary Resource *(Rajaresurssi)*

Boundary resources are, for instance, software tools and regulations that serve as the interface for the arm's-length relationship between the platform owner and the application developer. Boundary resources enable scalability and can be seen as two types: collaborative and technical. Collaborative boundary resources are, in practice, agreements and guidelines between the platform owner and the service provider attached to it. These include: instructions and guides, documentation, intangible capital (IPR) agreements, training materials, and online forums. Collaborative boundary resources transfer information between the parties and enable interaction between the platform and the developers. Technical boundary resources, for example, are APIs, SDKs, entire development environments, debugging tools, and compiler software for revealing and expanding the architecture of the platform.

Business Model *(Liiketoimintamalli)*

Business model articulates the logic, data, and other evidence that support a value proposition for the customer and a viable structure of revenues and costs for the enterprise delivering that value.

Business Model Canvas *(Liiketoimintamallityökalu)*

A tool that can be used to describe, analyze, and design business models.

Cloud Platform *(Pilvialusta)*

A platform that provides solutions for running different applications (e.g., data storage, machine learning, cognitive services) and almost unlimited resources for executing these solutions.

Developer Community *(Kehittäjäyhteisö, Hyödyntäjäyhteisö)*

A virtual community of application developers who use interfaces and cooperate with the API provider.

Developer Experience *(Kehittäjäkokemus)*

A developer's understanding of the development environment, as well as a sense of their own work and its importance as part of the whole.

DevOps *(DevOps)*

A collaborative cultural and operational model for the ability of high-performance IT to achieve one's business goals.

Digital Platform *(Digitaalinen alusta)*

A management system that controls, interacts with, and process data and external resources.

Digital Service *(Digitaalinen palvelu)*

A mobile application, e-commerce platform, website, online service, game, hardware, or, more broadly, the transmission or processing of digital information such as video viewing, streaming of television broadcasting, or file distribution. Most often, these services are used by people, not machines.

Ecosystem *(Ekosysteemi)*

Ecosystem is a new structure of economic relationships that enables the complementary production and/or consumption to be contained and coordinated without the need for vertical integration.

Endpoint *(Päätepiste)*

The API URL to which parameters can be attached and which

returns the response to the requestor. The endpoint may offer a variable number of CRUD methods.

GraphQL *(GraphQL)*

An open source question-based interface technology originally developed by Facebook. It challenges the REST software architecture but on the other hand can utilize the REST API layer in the background.

Hackathon *(Hackathon)*

A computer programming event or competition that introduces prototypes of digital innovations. Hackathons unite programmers and other professionals to work closely together for a short time to get ideas and resources for software projects for further development.

Integration *(Integraatio)*

Enterprise Application Integration (EAI) or systems integration where data is typically transferred between two different systems. Often includes data transfer and conversion.

Internal API *(Sisäinen API)*

API for use by organization-managed systems. In addition, one can split into private vs. internal API. See also *private API*.

JavaScript Object Notation (JSON)

A text syntax that facilitates structured data transfer between all programming languages. Offers a lighter and bracketed syntax as an alternative to XML and can be used in many connections, profiles, and applications.

JSON Web Token *(JWT)*

A compact, URL-safe way to transfer identifiers between two parties.

Machine Learning *(Koneoppiminen)*

An area of artificial intelligence that aims to make the software function better with the help of previous knowledge and possibly also user activity.

Microservice *(Mikropalvelu)*

An independently developed and managed application that can provide its services through API or REST API programming language.

Minimum Viable Product *(MVP)*

A product with just enough features to satisfy early customers and to provide feedback for future product development. An MVP emphasizes the speed of learning in development processes.

Network Effect *(Verkostovaikutus)*

Network effect means that the benefit to a person depends on the number of users. There are two main types of network effects: direct and indirect network effects. In the API economy, indirect network effects emphasize the provision of compatible and complementary services and applications.

OAuth2 *(OAuth2)*

A protocol used for authorization. See also OpenID Connect.

Open API *(Avoin API, avoin rajapinta)*

A classification that includes both public interfaces and partner interfaces.

Open API Specification *(Open API määrittely)*

A popular machine-readable de facto standard for API functionality and data models. Development takes place under the Linux Foundation.

Open Data Interface *(Avoimen datan rajapinta)*

Interfaces (REST APIs or others) used only to provide open data content.

OpenID Connect *(OpenID Connect)*

OpenID Connect 1.0 is a simple identity layer on top of the OAuth 2.0 protocol. It allows clients to verify the identity of the end-user based on the authentication performed by an authorization server, as well as to obtain basic profile information about the end-user in an interoperable and REST-like manner. OpenID Connect uses OAuth 2.0, which is a built-in authentication protocol that provides the ability to identify end-users and obtain additional information about them as REST. Utilizes JSON Web Token technology and is particularly well suited for services utilizing REST architecture that uses JSON data.

Open Source Software (OSS) (Avoimen lähdekoodin ohjelmisto)

Software that anyone can freely use, modify, and distribute in either a custom or unchanged format. Open source programs are collaborated on with many people and distributed under licenses that comply with open source principles.

Open Web Application Security Project (OWASP)

A world-wide nonprofit organization that publishes security checklists and instructions such as a REST API Cheat Sheet.

Partner API (Kumppani-API)

An API for a restricted group of external users. Usually provided between organizations, where the goal is to grow business or streamline processes.

Platform (Alusta)

A platform that enables interaction between platform users and producers that utilizes out-of-the-box resources and is often a digital solution.

Platform Economy (Alustatalous)

A set of initiatives that intermediate decentralized exchanges among peers through digital platforms. As a business model, platform economy is based on dynamic, multi-party innovation cooperation and exchange marketplaces, where it is possible to achieve wide-spreading and rapidly scalable network effects.

Plugin (Liitännäinen)

A technical extension for application operation. Deployment does not require code-level changes.

Private API (Yksityinen API)

An API used, for example, by its own mobile application; however, it is used on the open internet and therefore requires more protection.

Productization *(Tuotteistaminen)*

The crystallization of a service and its value by describing and standardizing various parts.

Public API *(Julkinen API)*

An API that may be used by external parties such as customers or partners of an organization. Charges may apply.

Resource *(Resurssi)*

Technical definition: anything one can refer to in the internet via a URL. Business definition: production factors, such as cognitive, personal, organizational, information, physical, financial, regulatory, and relationship resources.

Representational Stateless Transfer *API (REST API)*

The RESTful or Representational Stateless Transfer web service is an architectural model in which resources on the internet can be invoked occasionally over HTTP using HTTP methods.

Schema *(Skeema)*

An outline that describes the relationship between information and its parts. The schema can define mandatory fields and data types and can be used for automatic message checking; for example, JSON or XML schema or schema.org datatypes for linked data.

Script *(Skripti)*

A small piece of programming code that can be used, for example, to call interfaces.

Service Architecture (SOA) *(Palveluarkkitehtuuri)*

An architecture paradigm where data and functions are modeled as general and shared services. Previously, implementations were often made as a SOAP web service, but SOA can also be implemented; for example, REST API with HTTP.

Software Development Kit (SDK) *(Ohjelmistokehityspaketti)*

A collection of tools, libraries, relevant documents, code samples, processes, and instructions that allow developers to create software applications on a specific platform.

Single Page Architecture (SPA) *(SPA-arkkitehtuuri)*

One-page architecture with all functionality located on one page. For functions, the entire page is not reloaded; only the necessary parts are updated.

Token *(Token)*

A unique identifier used to identify API calls; for example, using the OpenID Connect standard. See also *JWT*.

Uniform Resource Identifier *(URI)*

A string that refers to an abstract or physical resource. The most popular is the URL.

Uniform Resource Locator *(URL)*

A string and syntax used to communicate the location of information on the internet.

Universally Unique Identifier *(UUID)*

A 128-bit globally unique string that establishes identity for information systems.

Value Creation *(Arvonluonti)*

The ways in which API generates value for customers, owners, and other stakeholders. An API can be a product itself or an enabling factor as part of a client's own value creation.

Value Proposition *(Arvolupaus)*

The benefits and disadvantages that an API provides to certain user groups. Answers the question why an API exists. Generally used in service and product development.

Value Proposition Canvas ***(Arvolupaus-työkalu)***

A tool for structuring a customer's needs and formulating a product or service concept to meet this need.

REFERENCES

Internet references are referenced on February 10th, 2019.

---

[1] http://team.finland.fi/artikkeli/-/asset_publisher/suomi-voi-kohota-alustatalouden-ja-tekoalyn-edellakavijamaaksi and http://valtioneuvosto.fi/artikkeli/-/asset_publisher/10616/alustatalous-suomen-kilpailutekijaksi-teollisuus-rohkeasti-mukaan-mallia-kasvu-yrityksista

[2] https://www.tivi.fi/Kaikki_uutiset/api-tuo-rahaa-rajapinnoista-uusi-nokia-6678493

[3] Ailisto, H. – Collin, J. – Juhanko, J. – Mäntylä, M. – Ruutu, S. –Seppälä, T. – Halén, M. – Hiekkanen, K. – Hyytinen, K. – Kiuru, E. – Korhonen, H. – Kääriäinen, J. – Parviainen, P. – Talvitie, J. (2016). Onko Suomi jäämässä alustatalouden junasta? Valtioneuvoston selvitys- ja tutkimustoiminnan julkaisusarja Nro 19/2016.

[4] Huhtamäki, J. – Basole, R.C. – Still, K. – Russell, M. – Seppänen, M. (2017). Visualizing the Geography of Platform Boundary Resources: The case of the Global API Ecosystem. Proceedings of HICSS-50, Hawaii, January 2017.

[5] Ajila, S. – Wu, D. (2007). Empirical study of the effects of open source adoption on software development economics. Journal of Systems and Software 80(9) s. 1517–1529.

[6] Example of a reference implementation, see https://github.com/6aika/api-linked-events

[7] https://pages.apigee.com/rs/apigee/images/APIs-not-integration-ebook-05-2014.pdf; https://history.apievangelist.com/

[8] https://aws.amazon.com/blogs/compute/monetize-your-apis-in-aws-marketplace-using-api-gateway/

[9] Hereafter, interface is used as a synonym for application programming interface (API)

[10] https://bbvaopen4u.com/en/actualidad/apis-books-amazon-google-books-isbn-and-their-open-apis

[11] http://toc.oreilly.com/2013/02/a-publishers-job-is-to-provide-a-good-api-for-books.html

[12] Apps (that is, mobile or web applications) use APIs to share information with backend system and data storages or to conduct e.g. calculations or text analyses as requested.

[13] https://www.kesko.fi/media/uutiset-ja-tiedotteet/uutiset/2016/kehittajat-innostuivat-keskon-haasteesta-digitaalisessa-innovointi- tapahtumassa7

[14] https://www.tivi.fi/Kaikki_uutiset/kesko-saa-apista-apua-ilman-rajapintoja-sovelluksen-kehitys-olisi-ollut-todella-haasta- vaa-6678685

[15] https://www.tivi.fi/Kaikki_uutiset/s-ryhma-rakentaa-api-kerroksen-6689051

[16] https://www.s-kanava.fi/web/s-ryhma/uutinen/helpompia-ja-hauskempia-ruokaostoksia-s-ryhma-ja-digital-foodie-solmivat-yhteistyosopimuksen/132628_66560

[17] http://www.digitalgoodie.com/enterworks-holding-company-invests-in-and-joins-with-leading-on-demand-grocery-platform-digital-foodie/

[18] https://www.kesko.fi/en/media/news-and-releases/press-releases/2017/k-group-enters-into-cooperation-with-alibaba-to-open-a-food-online-store-in-china/

[19] More on platform-based business and interfaces in Chapter 4.

[20] http://www.kaleva.fi/uutiset/talous/asiantuntija-verkkokauppa-kurittaa-perinteisia-kauppoja-varsinkin-jos-brandi-on-epaselva/748403/

[21] https://www.viestintavirasto.fi/viestintavirasto/blogit/2017/mat-kaketjujenhankintahelpoksi.html

[22] More on developer experience in Chapters 10 and 16.

[23] https://www.finextra.com/newsarticle/31141/canadian-lenders-is-sue-open-banking-warning

[24] Modified Woodall, T. (2003). Conceptualising 'value for the customer': An attributional, structural and dispositional analysis. Academy of Marketing Science Review.

[25] Woodall, T. (2003). Conceptualising 'value for the customer': An attributional, structural and dispositional analysis. Academy of Marketing Science Review.

[26] Modified Woodall, T. (2003). Conceptualising 'value for the customer': An attributional, structural and dispositional analysis. Academy of Marketing Science Review.

[27] Modified Kostamovaara, Henry, 2007. Utilizing a company's innovations: exploring customer value in three technology transfer cases. Master Thesis. Tampere University of Technology. 97 pages.

[28] Note that a customer means here a person who uses API

[29] https://strategyzer.com/canvas/value-proposition-canvas

[30] Smith, G. – Ofe, H. A. – Sandberg, J. (2016). Digital service innovation from open data: Exploring the value proposition of an open data marketplace. In System Sciences (HICSS), 2016 49th Hawaii International Conference on (s. 1277–1286). IEEE.

[31] http://api-as-a-product.com/articles/api-vpi-value-proposition-interface/

[32] Mäkinen – Dedehayir, 2013; in more detail Han, J. – Lowik, S., – de Weerd-Nederhof, P. (2017). Uncovering the conceptual boundaries of the ecosystems: Origins, evolution and future directions.

[33] "The ecosystem is defined by the alignment structure of the multilateral set of partners that need to interact in order for a focal value proposition to materialize. " Adner, R. (2017). Ecosystem as structure: An actionable construct for strategy. Journal of Management, 43(1), 39–58.

[34] Messerschmitt, D. G., – Szyperski, C. (2005). Software ecosystem: understanding an indispensable technology and industry. MIT Press Books, 1. In more detail about different types of ecosystems, please see Seppänen, M. – Hyrynsalmi, S. – Manikas, K. – Suominen, A. (2017). Yet another ecosystem literature review: 10+ 1 research communities. In Technology and Engineering Management Summit (E-TEMS), 2017 IEEE European (s. 1–8). IEEE. https://doi.org/10.1109/E-TEMS.2017.8244229

[35] Hyrynsalmi, S. – Seppänen, M. – Nokkala, T. – Suominen, A. – Järvi, A. (2015). Wealthy, Healthy and/or Happy—What does 'ecosystem health' stand for? In International Conference of Software Business (s. 272–287). Springer, Cham.

[36] Parker, G. G. – Van Alstyne, M. W. – Choudary, S. P. (2016). *Platform revolution. How networked markets are transforming the economy and how to make them work for you.*

[37] Choudary, S. P. (2015) *Platform Scale: How an emerging business model helps startups build large empires with minimum investment.* Platform Thinking Labs.

[38] Kim, W. C. – Mauborgne, R. A. (2014). *Blue ocean strategy: How to create uncontested market space and make the competition irrelevant.* Harvard business review Press.

[39] Huhtamäki, J. – Basole, R. – Still, K. – Russell, M. – Seppänen, M. (2017). Visualizing the Geography of Platform Boundary Resources:

The Case of the Global API Ecosystem. In Proceedings of the 50th Hawaii International Conference on System Sciences.

[40] Basole, R. C. (2016). Accelerating Digital Transformation: Visual Insights from the API Ecosystem. IT Professional, 18(6), 20–25. https://ieeexplore.ieee.org/document/7763725/

[41] https://www.programmableweb.com/

[42] http://apis.io/

[43] https://rapidapi.com/

[44] https://apis.guru/openapi-directory/

[45] More information about API catalog, see https://nordicapis.com/api-discovery-15-ways-to-find-apis/

[46] Huotari, P. (2017). "Strategic interaction in platform-based markets: An agent-based simulation approach." Acta Universitatis Lappeenrantaensis

[47] Weiss, M. – Gangadharan, G. R. (2010). "Modeling the mashup ecosystem: Structure and growth." R&D Management 40.1: 40–49.

[48] Korhonen, H. M. E. – Still, K. – Seppänen, M. – Kumpulainen, M. – Suominen, A. – Valkokari, K. (2017). The Core Interaction of Platforms: How Startups Connect Users and Producers. Technology Innovation Management Review, 7(9): 17–29.

[49] Van Alstyne, M. W. – Parker, G. G. – Choudary, S. P. (2016). Pipelines, platforms, and the new rules of strategy. Harvard Business Review, 94(4), 54–62.

[50] Dal Bianco, V. et al. (2014). "The role of platform boundary resources in software ecosystems: a case study." Software Architecture (WICSA), 2014 IEEE/IFIP Conference on. IEEE.

[51] McPhee, C. – Dedehayir, O. – Seppänen, M. (2017). Editorial: Platforms and Ecosystems. Technology Innovation Management Review, 7(9): 3–5.

[52] Botsman, R. (2017). Who Can You Trust? How Technology Brought Us Together and Why It Might Drive Us Apart. Public Affairs.

[53] See e.g., Parker, G. G. – Van Alstyne, M. W. – Choudary, S. P. (2016). Platform Revolution: How Networked Markets Are Transforming the Economy – and How to Make Them Work for You.

[54] Smedlund, A. – Faghankhani, H. (2015). Platform Orchestration for Efficiency, Development, and Innovation. In System Sciences (HICSS), 2015 48th Hawaii International Conference on (s. 1380–1388). IEEE.

[55] http://www.olx.com

[56] https://www.forbes.com/sites/louiscolumbus/2017/01/29/2017-is-quickly-becoming-the-year-of-the-api-eco-nomy/#1d6fa5d66a4

[57] Still, K. – Valkokari, K. - Seppänen, M. – Huhtamäki, J. - Seppälä, T. – Basole, R. - Gawer, A. (Oct 31, 2017). " Platform Economy – Interactions & Boundary Resources: Checklist For Companies". ETLA Memo No 62. https://www.etla.fi/wp-content/uploads/INTERACTIONS_BOUNDARY_RESOURCES_CHECKLIST_2017_10_27.pdf

[58] For an overview, see: https://hbr.org/cover-story/2017/07/the-business-of-artificial-intelligence; https://janiwahlman.com/2017/08/03/tekoaly-koneoppiminen-ja-liiketoiminta/; Schmidhuber, J. (2015). Deep learning in neural networks: An overview. Neural networks, 61, 85–117.

[59] https://www.etla.fi/julkaisut/the-application-of-artificial-intelligence-at-chinese-digital-platform-giants-baidu-alibaba-and-tencent/

[60] O'Reilly, T. (2007). What Is Web 2.0: Design Patterns and Business Models for the Next Generation of Software https://mpra.ub.uni-muenchen.de/4578/1/mpra_paper_4578.pdf

[61] Script is a short section of code that may be used to call interfaces.

[62] Open source solutions like OpenHAB and solutions offered by big cloud companies like AWS, Google, Samsung and IBM are extending compatibility to devices by various technology providers.

[63] Mercedes-Benz has published marketing interfaces in 2017 and a smart car API in 2018. Volvo has developed internal APIs for some years.

[64] User communities of Tesla and Volkswagen have craved for open APIs long before the companies have decided to provide them.

[65] https://thenewstack.io/lessons-learned-from-hacking-the-tesla-api/

[66] For a list of them, see: http://www.goodnewsfinland.com/feature/finland-makes-iot-connection/

[67] Richardson, L. – Ruby, S. (2007). RESTful Web Services, s. 81.

[68] Fielding, R. T., - Taylor, R. N. (2002). Principled design of the modern Web architecture. ACM Transactions on Internet Technology (TOIT), 2(2), 115-150. https://www.ics.uci.edu/~fielding/pubs/webarch_icse2000.pdf

[69] For those looking for a more technical explanations: Products API, with endpoint "/products" used with HTTP-methods to add (POST /products), retrieve (GET /products) or remove (DELETE /products) products.

[70] Seppänen, M. (2009). Empirical classification of resources in a business model concept. Intangible Capital, 5(2), s. 102–124.

[71] Seppänen, M. – Mäkinen, S. (2007). Towards a classification of resources for the business model concept. International Journal of Management Concepts and Philosophy, 2(4): 389–404.

[72] Seppälä, T. et al. (2015). Digitaaliset alustat: kolmas aalto rantautuu – neljäs aalto nousee.

[73] API may be used as self-service when it is publicly available. Documentation, SDKs, test environments may be publicly available but in some cases, they may require connection to provider beforehand.

[74] https://bankinnovation.net/2017/09/braintree-four-years-post-the-paypal-acquisition/

[75] https://www.tekniikkatalous.fi/talous_uutiset/op-ostaa-mobiili-maksamisfirman-6673680

[76] Gassmann, O. – Frankenberger, K. – Csik, M. (2017). The St. Gallen Business Model Navigator. Working paper. University of St. Gallen.

[77] https://www.slideshare.net/jmusser/j-musser-apibizmodels2013; https://www.youtube.com/watch?v=e2OFCkGQcw8

[78] Hatvala, A. 2016. Open Innovation Opportunities and Business Benefits of Web APIs A Case Study of Finnish API Providers https://aaltodoc.aalto.fi/bitstream/handle/123456789/21446/hse_ethesis_14624.pdf?sequence=1&isAllowed=y

[79] Wulf, J. – Blohm, I. (2017). Service Innovation through Application Programming Interfaces-Towards a Typology of Service Designs.

[80] Benzell, S. – Lagarda, G. – Van Alstyne, M.W. (2017). The Impact of APIs in Firm Performance.

https://papers.ssrn.com/abstract=2843326

[81] Heinonen, K. – Strandvik, T. (2015). Customer-dominant logic: foundations and implications. Journal of Services Marketing. Vol. 29, Iss. 6/7, s. 472–484.

[82] http://apievangelist.com/2015/02/03/in-the-future-there-will-be-no-public-vs-private-apis/

[83] http://blog.restcase.com/internal-vs-external-apis/
https://www.3scale.net/2015/02/public-vs-private-vs-internal-apis/

[84] Benzell, S. – Lagarda, G. – Van Alstyne, M. W. (2017). The Impact of APIs in Firm Performance.

[85] More details on internal APIs in Chapter 7.

[86] https://www.cio.com/article/3218667/digital-transformation/have-you-had-your-bezos-moment-what-you-can-learn-from-amazon.html

[87] https://community.vismasolutions.com/docs/DOC-2669

[88] https://www.tekniikkatalous.fi/tekniikka/aly-tulee-hisseihin-nain-kone-aikoo-paihittaa-kilpailijansa-624447 Potential uses are illustrated with elevators communication, see http://machineconversations.kone.com/

[89] http://www.kone.com/en/stories-and-references/stories/decoding-the-connected-world.aspx

[90] https://www.statista.com/statistics/226927/alibaba-cumulative-active-online-buyers-taobao-tmall/

[91] This is an opposite way to see the saying "If we build it, they will come" that underlines that a good product is just enough. Markus, M. L. & Keil, M. (1994) "If we build it, they will come: Designing information systems that people want to use." Sloan Management Review 35.4, 11. 102 Anderson, C. (2013). Makers: The New Industrial Revolution,s. 143.

[92] https://tietosuojauutiset.fi/2016/05/19/julkisasiamies-myos-dynaamiset-ip-osoiteet-ovat-henkilotietoja/

[93] https://www.programmableweb.com/news/how-to-pick-best-business-models-your-apis/analysis/2017/09/27

[94] https://www.computerworld.com/article/2496465/enterprise-applications/open-your-data-to-the-world.html

[95] https://datahelpdesk.worldbank.org/knowledgebase/articles/889386-developer-information-overview

[96] https://developers.google.com/maps/pricing-and-plans/

[97] Lakomaa, E. – Kallberg, J. (2013). Open Data as a Foundation for Innovation: The Enabling Effect of free Public Sector Information for Entrepreneurs.

[98] http://platformed.info/country-as-a-platform-why-singapores-future-needs-a-platform-strategy/

[99] The Open Definition. Open Knowledge International. http://opendefinition.org/

[100] O'Reilly, T. (2011). Government as a platform. Innovations, s. 13–40.

[101] Bates, J. (2014). The strategic importance of information policy for the contemporary neoliberal state: The case of Open Government Data in the United Kingdom. Government Information Quarterly, s.388–395.

[102] http://avoinrajapinta.fi

[103] https://www.liikennevirasto.fi/avoindata/digiroad

[104] JHS 189 Avoimen tietoaineiston käyttölupa. http://docs.jhs-suositukset.fi/jhs-suositukset/JHS189/JHS189.html

[105] http://avp.aalto.fi/events/entrepreneurial-leadership-avp-master-class-by-marten-mickos/

[106] https://www.apiopscycles.com/api-canvas

[107] See for instance Deutsche Bank https://developer.db.com or Nordea Open Banking https://developer.nordeaopenbanking.com/

[108] Chesbrough, H. W. (2006). Open innovation: The new imperative for creating and profiting from technology. Harvard Business Press.

[109] Rogers, Everett M. (2010). Diffusion of innovations. 4th Edition.

[110] Moore, Geoffrey A. (2002). Crossing the chasm.

[111] Raymond, E. (1999) *"The cathedral and the bazaar" Knowledge,* Technology & Policy 12.3: 23–49.

[112] Minimum Viable Product, see more from https://www.techopedia.com/definition/27809/minimum-viable-product-mvp

[113] http://blog.ninlabs.com/2013/03/api-documentation/

[114] Tan, Wei et al. (2016). "From the service-oriented architecture to the web API economy." IEEE Internet Computing 20.4: 64–68.

[115] Bosch, J. – Bosch-Sijtsema, P. (2010). From integration to composition: On the impact of software product lines, global development and ecosystems. Journal of Systems and Software, 83(1), s. 67–76.

[116] Aitamurto, T. – Lewis, S.C. (2013). Open innovation in digital journalism: Examining the impact of Open APIs at four news organizations. New media & society, 15(2), s. 314–331.

[117] For more information please see http://www.scaledagileframework.com/features-and-components/

[118] http://apimanifesti.fi/

[119] http://agilemanifesto.org/

[120] https://www.apiopscycles.com

[121] https://www.twilio.com/docs/api

[122] https://stripe.com/docs

[123] https://developer.github.com/v3/

[124] https://sendgrid.com/docs/API_Reference/index.html

[125] https://www.programmableweb.com/news/10-reasons-why-developers-hate-your-api/2014/05/23

[126] http://www.syncdev.com/minimum-viable-product/

[127] Basili, V. R., Selby, R. W., & Hutchens, D. H. (1986). Experimentation in software engineering. IEEE Transactions on software engineering, (7), 733-743.

[128] Versioning does not automatically mean that API version number will grow.

[129] Shoup, R. (2014). Good Enough is Good Enough "Minimal Viable Architecture" in a Startup.

[130] https://www.wired.com/2015/09/google-2-billion-lines-code-and-one-place/

[131] See e.g. http://www.vaestoliitto.fi/media/graafinen_ohjeisto/ and https://www.hyvaasuomesta.fi/yrityksille/merkin-kayttosaan-not/graafinen-ohjeisto

[132] Fielding, R. T. – Taylor, R. N. (2000). Architectural styles and the design of network-based software architectures. Doctoral dissertation: University of California, Irvine.

[133] Masse, M. (2009). REST API Design Rulebook: Designing Consistent RESTful Web Service Interfaces. "O'Reilly Media, Inc.", 2011.

Robillard, M. P. "What Makes APIs Hard to Learn? Answers from Developers," IEEE Software, vol. 26, no. 6, s. 27–34.

[134] http://apistylebook.com/design/guidelines/

[135] Chen, Y. – Xu, X. – Zhu, L. (2012). "Web Platform API Design Principles and Service Contract," 2012 19th Asia-Pacific Software Engineering Conference, Hong Kong, s. 877–886.

[136] Krintz, C. – Jayathilaka, H. – Dimopoulos, S. – Pucher, A. – Wolski, R. – Bultan, T. (2014) "Cloud Platform Support for API Governance," 2014 IEEE International Conference on Cloud Engineering, Boston, MA, s. 615–618.

[137] https://restfulapi.net/versioning/ and https://developer.ibm.com/apiconnect/2014/11/06/api-versioning-managing-changes-api/

[138] For instance: Open API specification, http://openapis.org/

[139] https://apinf.gitbooks.io/api-guidelines/content/documentation.html

[140] Macvean, A.– Maly, M. – Daughtry, J. (2016). API Design Reviews at Scale. In Proceedings of the 2016 CHI Conference Extended Abstracts on Human Factors in Computing Systems (CHI EA '16). ACM, New York, NY, USA, 849–858.

[141] Nykaza, J. – Messinger, R. – Boehme, F. – Norman, C. L. – Mace,M. – Gordon, M. (2002). What programmers really want: results of a needs assessment for SDK documentation. In Proceedings of the 20th annual international conference on Computer documentation (SIGDOC '02). ACM, New York, NY, USA, 133–141.

[142] E.g. SwaggerHub includes automatically creation of mockup API. https://app.swaggerhub.com

[143] Robillard, M. P. (2009). "What Makes APIs Hard to Learn? Answers from Developers," in IEEE Software, vol. 26, no. 6, s. 27–34.

[144] https://www.owasp.org/index.php/REST_Security_Cheat_Sheet

[145] https://www.apiopscycles.com/api-audit

[146] http://www.rfc-base.org/rfc-4122.html

[147] E.g. hackr.fi and hackerone.com.

[148] http://dev.hsl.fi/graphql/console/ and http://api.digitransit.fi/graphiql/hsl

[149] HSL documentation how to set up local environment. https://digitransit.fi/en/developers/services/6-data-containers/geocoding-data/

[150] Robillard, M.P. (2009). "What Makes APIs Hard to Learn? Answers from Developers," in IEEE Software, vol. 26, no. 6, s. 27–34.

[151] Customer-centricity is also in focus in R&D. See e.g. Fader, P. (2012) Customer centricity: Focus on the right customers for strategic advantage. Wharton digital press.

[152] Puccinelli, N, M., et al. (2009). "Customer experience management in retailing: understanding the buying process." Journal of retailing 85.1 (2009): 15–30.

[153] Lemon, K. N. – Verhoef, P. C. (2016). "Understanding customer experience throughout the customer journey." Journal of Marketing 80.6 (2016): 69–96.

[154] Brynjolfsson, E. – Yu Jeffrey Hu – Rahman, M. S. (2013). "Competing in the age of omnichannel retailing." MIT Sloan Management Review 54.4 (2013): 23.

[155] Rawson, A. – Duncan, E. – Jones, C. (2013). "The truth about customer experience." Harvard Business Review 91.9 (2013): 90–98.

[156] https://stripe.com/docs/api

[157] Lemon, K. N. – Verhoef, P. C. (2016). "Understanding customer experience throughout the customer journey." Journal of Marketing 80.6 (2016): 69–96.

[158] Fagerholm, F. (2015) "Software Developer Experience: Case Studies in Lean-Agile and Open Source Environments"

[159] https://aws.amazon.com/marketplace/pp/B01N3NNLIW

[160] https://developer.nordeaopenbanking.com/

[161] https://op-developer.fi/

[162] Package management tool enabling distribution of software packages to other developers, for JavaScript packages: https://www.npmjs.com/

[163] Package management tool for Python developers: https://en.wikipedia.org/wiki/Pip_(package_manager)

[164] Ries, E. (2011). The Lean Startup. How Today's Entrepreneurs Use Continuous Innovation to Create Radically Successful Business.

[165] https://www.prh.fi/stc/attachments/PRH_Vuosikertomus_2015_fin_WWW.pdf

[166] Lwakatare, L. – Kuvaja, P. – Oivo, M. (2015). Dimensions of DevOps.

[167] https://nordicapis.com/is-graphql-the-end-of-rest-style-apis/

[168] https://medium.com/apiops/graphql-is-the-newer-kid-on-the-block-and-eats-apis-for-breakfast-or-even-replaces-the-need-for-9d7cd6eb2514

[169] Aziz, B. (2015). Web API Management Meets the Internet of Things. The Semantic Web: ESWC 2015 Satellite Events: ESWC 2015 Satellite Events, Portorož, Slovenia, May 31–June 4, 2015, Revised Selected Papers, 9341, p. 367.

[170] Most often used methods are GET, POST, PUT, DELETE, OPTIONS and HEAD.

[171] Di Francesco, P. – Malavolta, I. – Lago, P. (2017). Research on architecting microservices: Trends, focus, and potential for industrial adoption. In Software Architecture (ICSA), 2017 IEEE International Conference on (s. 21–30). IEEE.

[172] https://medium.com/@nathankpeck/microservice-principles-decentralized-governance-4cdbde2ff6ca

[173] Wingelhofer, R. – Aistleitner, M. (2017) September. Microservices in a Small Development Organization. In Software Architecture: 11th European Conference, ECSA 2017, Canterbury, UK, September 11-15, 2017, Proceedings (Vol. 10475, s. 208). Springer.

[174] Cuesta, E. C. – Navarro, E. – Zdun, U. (2018). Synergies of System-of-Systems and Microservices Architectures.

[175] Di Francesco, P. – Malavolta, I. – Lago, P. (2017). Research on architecting microservices: Trends, focus, and potential for industrial adoption. In Software Architecture (ICSA), 2017 IEEE International Conference on (s. 21–30). IEEE.

[176] Mili, H. – Shatnami, A. – Moha, N. – Privat, J. – Valtchev, P. – de Technologie, E. (2017). Service-Oriented Re-engineering of Legacy JEE Applications: Issues and Research Directions. http://www.latece.uqam.ca/wp-content/uploads/2017/10/rapport-17-6.pdf

[177] https://openid.net/connect/

[178] https://www.oasis-open.org/committees/tc_home.php?wg_abbrev=security

[179] Bazarhanova, A. – Yli-Huumo, J. – Smolander, K. (2018). Love and Hate Relationships in a Platform Ecosystem: A case of Finnish Electronic Identity Management. In Proceedings of the 51st Hawaii International Conference on System Sciences.

[180] Naik, N. – Jenkins, P. (2017). Securing digital identities in the cloud by selecting an opposite Federated Identity Management from SAML, OAuth and OpenID Connect. In Research Challenges in Information Science (RCIS), 2017 11th International Conference on (s. 163–174). IEEE.

CPSIA information can be obtained
at www.ICGtesting.com
Printed in the USA
LVHW011441170619
621463LV00016B/389

9 789528 008491